Sin Documentos

33 1/3 Global

33 1/3 Global, a series related to but independent from **33 1/3**, takes the format of the original series of short, music-based books and brings the focus to music throughout the world. With initial volumes focusing on Japanese and Brazilian music, the series will also include volumes on the popular music of Australia/Oceania, Europe, Africa, the Middle East, and more.

33 1/3 Japan

Series Editor: Noriko Manabe

Spanning a range of artists and genres – from the 1970s rock of Happy End to technopop band Yellow Magic Orchestra, the Shibuya-kei of Cornelius, classic anime series *Cowboy Bebop*, J-Pop/EDM hybrid Perfume, and vocaloid star Hatsune Miku—33 1/3 Japan is a series devoted to in-depth examination of Japanese popular music of the twentieth and twenty-first centuries.

Published Titles:

Supercell's *Supercell* by Keisuke Yamada

Yoko Kanno's *Cowboy Bebop Soundtrack* by Rose Bridges

Perfume's *Game* by Patrick St. Michel

Cornelius's *Fantasma* by Martin Roberts

Joe Hisaishi's *My Neighbor Totoro: Soundtrack* by Kunio Hara

Shonen Knife's *Happy Hour* by Brooke McCorkle

Nenes' *Koza Dabasa* by Henry Johnson

Yuming's *The 14th Moon* by Lasse Lehtonen

Forthcoming Titles:

Yellow Magic Orchestra's *Yellow Magic Orchestra* by Toshiyuki Ohwada

Kohaku utagassen: The Red and White Song Contest by Shelley Brunt

33 1/3 Brazil

Series Editor: Jason Stanyek

Covering the genres of samba, tropicália, rock, hip hop, forró, bossa nova, heavy metal and funk, among others, 33 1/3 Brazil is a series devoted to in-depth examination of the most important Brazilian albums of the twentieth and twenty-first centuries.

Published Titles:
Caetano Veloso's *A Foreign Sound* by Barbara Browning
Tim Maia's *Tim Maia Racional Vols. 1 &2* by Allen Thayer
João Gilberto and Stan Getz's *Getz/Gilberto* by Brian McCann
Gilberto Gil's *Refazenda* by Marc A. Hertzman
Dona Ivone Lara's *Sorriso Negro* by Mila Burns
Milton Nascimento and Lô Borges's *The Corner Club* by Jonathon Grasse
Racionais MCs' *Sobrevivendo no Inferno* by Derek Pardue
Naná Vasconcelos's *Saudades* by Daniel B. Sharp
Chico Buarque's First *Chico Buarque* by Charles A. Perrone

Forthcoming Titles:
Jorge Ben Jor's *África Brasil* by Frederick J. Moehn

33 1/3 Europe

Series Editor: Fabian Holt
Spanning a range of artists and genres, 33 1/3 Europe offers engaging accounts of popular and culturally significant albums of Continental Europe and the North Atlantic from the twentieth and twenty-first centuries.

Published Titles:
Darkthrone's *A Blaze in the Northern Sky* by Ross Hagen
Ivo Papazov's *Balkanology* by Carol Silverman
Heiner Müller and Heiner Goebbels's *Wolokolamsker Chaussee* by Philip V. Bohlman
Modeselektor's *Happy Birthday!* by Sean Nye
Mercyful Fate's *Don't Break the Oath* by Henrik Marstal
Bea Playa's *I'll Be Your Plaything* by Anna Szemere and András Rónai
Various Artists' *DJs do Guetto* by Richard Elliott

Czesław Niemen's *Niemen Enigmatic* by Ewa Mazierska and Mariusz
     Gradowski
Massada's *Astaganaga* by Lutgard Mutsaers
Los Rodríguez's *Sin Documentos* by Héctor Fouce and Fernán del Val

Forthcoming Titles:
Nuovo Canzoniere Italiano's *Bella Ciao* by Jacopo Tomatis
Amália Rodrigues's *Amália at the Olympia* by Lilla Ellen Gray
Ardit Gjebrea's *Projekt Jon* by Nicholas Tochka
Vopli Vidopliassova's *Tantsi* by Maria Sonevytsky
Édith Piaf's *Recital 1961* by David Looseley
Iannis Xenakis' *Persepolis* by Aram Yardumian

33 1/3 Oceania

Series Editors: Jon Stratton (senior editor) and Jon Dale (specializing in
     books on albums from Aotearoa/New Zealand)
Spanning a range of artists and genres from Australian Indigenous
artists to Maori and Pasifika artists, from Aotearoa/New Zealand noise
music to Australian rock, and including music from Papua and other
Pacific islands, 33 1/3 Oceania offers exciting accounts of albums that
illustrate the wide range of music made in the Oceania region.

Published Titles:
John Farnham's *Whispering Jack* by Graeme Turner
The Church's *Starfish* by Chris Gibson
Regurgitator's *Unit* by Lachlan Goold and Lauren Istvandity

Forthcoming Titles:
Ed Kuepper's *Honey Steel's Gold* by John Encarnacao
Kylie Minogue's *Kylie* by Adrian Renzo and Liz Giuffre
Space Waltz's *Space Waltz* by Ian Chapman
The Dead C's *Clyma est mort* by Darren Jorgensen
Chain's *Toward the Blues* by Peter Beilharz
Bic Runga's *The Drive* by Henry Johnson
The Front Lawn's *Songs from the Front Lawn* by Matthew Bannister

Sin Documentos

Héctor Fouce and Fernán del Val

Series Editor: Fabian Holt

BLOOMSBURY ACADEMIC

NEW YORK · LONDON · OXFORD · NEW DELHI · SYDNEY

BLOOMSBURY ACADEMIC
Bloomsbury Publishing Inc
1385 Broadway, New York, NY 10018, USA
50 Bedford Square, London, WC1B 3DP, UK
29 Earlsfort Terrace, Dublin 2, Ireland

BLOOMSBURY, BLOOMSBURY ACADEMIC and the Diana logo
are trademarks of Bloomsbury Publishing Plc

First published in the United States of America 2023

A catalog record for this book is available from the Library of Congress.

ISBN: HB: 978-1-5013-5788-6
PB: 978-1-5013-5789-3
ePDF: 978-1-5013-5791-6
eBook: 978-1-5013-5790-9

Typeset by Newgen KnowledgeWorks Pvt. Ltd., Chennai, India
Printed and bound in Great Britain

Series: 33 1/3 Europe

To find out more about our authors and books visit www.bloomsbury.com
and sign up for our newsletters.

Contents

Introduction

Global and hybrid: Los Rodríguez and Spanish pop

Estar de Rodríguez: Idiom used in Spain to refer to a husband who is left alone in the city while his family is on vacation, working but often having fun at the end of the day.

This book aims to reflect on how Los Rodríguez, and their album *Sin Documentos*, challenged the dominant way of understanding the globalization of rock. The analysis of this album offers an opportunity to reflect on the global circulation of pop and rock music and to understand how these genres have taken root in Spain's national culture and have mixed with local sounds, slang and accents.

The name of the band, Los Rodríguez, reflects a straightforward view of popular themes and a foreign perspective, with a touch of irony, on traditional Spanish culture. According to the most recent biography of the band (Babas and Turrón 2020), when singer Andrés Calamaro (b. 1961, Buenos Aires) had just arrived in Madrid from Argentina, he asked about the meaning of the idiom *estar de Rodríguez* after hearing it in the street. The phrase, popularized in some very successful films of the sixties, refers to a married city man who stays behind in the city while his family goes on a summer vacation to the coast or the village, with the excuse of having to work, to have some fun while his wife and children are away. Those family-free days would be used to get out of control, go out, pick up women and do everything that a good husband should not do in the Catholic Spain of the sixties (at least not when the family was around). This male archetype was celebrated in popular films produced in the late sixties and early seventies (prior to the death of the dictator Francisco Franco in 1975), such as *El cálido verano del Sr. Rodríguez* (The Hot Summer of Mr. Rodríguez) (Pedro Lazaga, 1965), starring José Luis López Vázquez (1922–2009), the actor who could best represent that dull, repressed, bald-headed and moustachioed Spanish office worker.[1]

Andrés Calamaro loved this idiom and proposed it as the name of the band he was beginning to assemble with Ariel Rot (b.1960, Buenos Aires), Germán Vilella (b.1964, Madrid) and Julián Infante (b.1957, Ciudad Real; d.2000, Madrid): Los Rodríguez. Everyone who heard this proposed name for the band was horrified, considering the phrase to be tacky, old-fashioned and boring. Despite this reaction, the band went ahead with the idea. This decision reveals that Calamaro had a nose to detect the greatness of the everyday, popular and costumbrist[2] aspects of popular culture and integrate them into his songs.

In Spain, the surname *Rodríguez* is among the most common and ordinary, like the characters embodied by López Vázquez. Nonetheless, it was a popular surname, just like Los Rodríguez: a popular, well-liked and respected band, whose songs were played at all local festivals. Los Rodríguez were capable of creating memorable songs that became part of Spanish popular culture. The hedonistic, *carpe diem* connotations of the phrase *estar de Rodríguez* also fit with the band's idiosyncrasies: the shirts with flamenco motifs that its members wore in concerts and promotional photos, their sceptical attitude towards relationships and quotidian life and their predilection for traditional bars, such as El Palentino.[3]

The band emerged in 1990 when four musicians with experience in musical scenes on both sides of the Atlantic decided to join forces. Andrés Calamaro was a well-known and experienced Argentine musician who had played keyboards in the candombe-rock band Raíces (Roots) and in Los Abuelos de la Nada (The Grandparents of Nothingness), a landmark band in the history of Argentina's national rock scene, with whom he composed the 1983 hit song 'Mil horas' (A Thousand Hours). Calamaro had already carved out a solo career of four albums, the last two made in collaboration with Ariel Rot. The latter had made his musical career in Spain, where he arrived in the mid-seventies after his father, a journalist, was threatened by the Argentine dictatorship. Rot teamed up with Alejo Stivel (b. 1959, Buenos Aires), who was born and raised in Argentina, in Tequila, a band that enjoyed great success in the late seventies, the first years of the Spanish Transition[4] to democracy. Tequila created rock music that took inspiration from the Rolling Stones and New Wave music. After the members of Tequila disbanded, Rot released two solo albums that received little recognition, then returned to Argentina, where he met Calamaro.

Julián Infante, the rhythm guitarist of the group, was also a former member of Tequila and had enjoyed great recognition in the Spanish rock scene as part of such bands as Glutamato Ye-Yé, Desperados, Pistones, Academia Parabüten and Martirio. As of this writing, Infante is the only member of the band who is no longer living. Finally, Germán Vilella, the band's drummer, is the son of a Puerto Rican father and a Spanish mother. He spent his childhood and adolescence in the United States and Spain and gained extensive experience, from a very young age, working in diverse scenes with such musicians as Mercedes Ferrer, Antonio Flores, Luz Casal, Luis Eduardo Aute and Álex & Christina.

The band's discography was short but intense: in less than a decade of life, they produced four albums and one compilation. Their first two albums went unnoticed as they were released by small record labels that received little support from major radio stations, which were the main vehicle for the promotion of music in those years. With *Sin Documentos*, however, the band managed to attract DRO Records, the main Spanish independent record label, which had been acquired by the multinational Warner at the end of the eighties. This album was strongly supported and was well received by critics and audiences alike. The title track of the album, in a sort of rumba-rock style, has become part of the Spanish cultural imaginary: it is commonly included on critics' lists of best Spanish pop songs[5] and is still played in the Spanish *verbenas*.[6] The double appeal of Los Rodríguez, getting praise from critics and from the general public and being played in rock bars and local festivals, made them a *rara avis* within the Spanish rock scene. This allowed them to take certain risks that native Spanish rock bands did not dare to take and helped them to transcend the limits and borders of music scenes and genres.

In short, Los Rodríguez have had a huge impact on Spanish popular music. The success of *Sin Documentos* was repeated with the following album, *Palabras más, palabras menos* (Give or Take a Word or Two), whose first single 'Milonga del marinero y el capitán' (The Milonga of the Sailor and the Captain) solidified the band's commitment to mix rock and Latin folk music. This path was later taken by multiple bands (such as La

Cabra Mecánica, Estopa, El Canto del Loco, El Hombre Gancho, Los Cucas or Pereza) throughout the nineties and into the early twenty-first century. However, the legacy of Los Rodríguez can also be observed beyond the musical realm, in the lyrical dimension. Calamaro's lyrics approached emotional issues, love and heartbreak in a way that was closer to the work of melodic singers than to that of rock bands, which in turn opened up a wider range of themes and topics for musicians and songwriters. In addition to the aforementioned bands, many singer-songwriters and bands can be said to be influenced by Calamaro's songwriting style (e.g. Quique González, Leiva, Fabián D. Cuesta, Xoel López or Iván Ferreiro).

As we said before, Los Rodríguez and their album *Sin Documentos* are an interesting object to reflect how rock music has been globalized. For Israeli sociologist Motti Regev (2013), rock is an example of aesthetic cosmopolitanism: various elements of popular culture (film, music, television, etc.) have become globalized, but have had to adopt traits and patterns of the receiving cultures in the process. What Regev proposes is an amendment to the theories of globalization as cultural homogenization. He argues that popular music genres, such as rock, have been adapted to and hybridized with the representative music, instruments, slang, clichés and accents of the receiving cultures, thus becoming cultural elements of their own. As examples, Regev mentions Almendra in Argentina, Ehud Banai in Israel, Cui Jian in China, Noir Désir in France and Os Mutantes in Brazil, among many others. Thus, to be global, rock has to be local.

In that sense, since the sixties, Spanish pop-rock has substantiated Regev's theories. One example of this is Los Pekenikes and their 1964 version, influenced by the Shadows, of 'Los cuatro muleros' (The Four Muleteers), a popular song of the early twentieth century that poet Federico García Lorca had included in his compilation of Andalusian folk songs. Another is Los Brincos, a band that emerged after the success of the Beatles and combined beat rock with an aesthetic close to the Spanish *tuna*,[7] introducing typical flamenco scales and sounds in some of their songs.

In the seventies, Spain witnessed the development of various music scenes that mixed hybridized progressive rock and hard rock with folk music, such as flamenco, rumba and sardana.[8] Especially relevant here are the so-called flamenco rock and gypsy rock bands that emerged in Andalusia. Groups like Veneno, Alameda and Triana sang with an Andalusian accent, incorporated *quejíos*,[9] played blues with Spanish guitars and applied typical flamenco structures to progressive rock. In the eighties, marked by punk and New Wave, other bands (e.g. Gabinete Caligari) also combined the rhythmic structure of *pasodoble*[10] with rock, used castanets and sang about the life of bullfighters like Juan Belmonte. These hybridization dynamics have prevailed over time with such bands as Los Coyotes, El Último de la Fila, Radio Futura, La Cabra Mecánica, Estopa, Amparanoia or Manu Chao, and have contributed to the success of Spanish global stars including Rosalía and C. Tangana, whose music combines current musical genres (trap, rap, electronic, reggaeton) with flamenco and rumba.

In this process of stylistic evolution and hybridization, the pattern seems to be a circulation from the centre to the periphery, where musical innovations always come from the rock metropolises of the United States and Great Britain. After the Beatles and later Jethro Tull emerged in Great Britain, Spanish imitations appeared in the form of Los Brincos and Ñu, respectively. Likewise, the groups Barón Rojo and Obús were launched in Spain after the birth of the new wave of British heavy metal.

This model of pop-rock globalization, from the centre to the periphery – 'Let others do the inventing and we will take advantage of their inventions', to paraphrase Miguel de Unamuno[11] – is precisely what Los Rodríguez and significant elements of Spanish popular music have challenged. This is because innovations in Spanish popular music have not only come from the two metropolises of Great Britain and the United States. Instead, neighbouring European countries (like France and Italy) as well as Latin American countries have also made cultural exchanges of great importance. The scarce historiography of Spanish pop-rock (Domínguez 2002; Marc 2013; Ordovás 1987; Pardo 2005) has made this point, but it is necessary to further investigate it to evaluate the significance of an album like *Sin Documentos.*

It should be noted that the arrival of rock and roll to Spain is linked to the Pactos de Madrid (Madrid Pacts) signed by Francoist Spain and the United States in 1953, which allowed the establishment of four American military bases on Spanish territory, in Torrejón de Ardoz (Madrid), Zaragoza, Morón (Seville) and Rota (Cádiz), and ended the international isolation Spain had received as a punishment for supporting the Axis powers. The bases became a space for the dissemination of North American culture, thanks to commercial exchanges and contact in the streets between the Spanish and foreign populations. As Ignacio Faulín (2016) points out, it is also necessary to take into account the fact that North American music had been present in Spanish culture since the nineteenth century. Record labels were used to releasing albums from the United States, and the jazz and blues music scenes in Spain were well established (Iglesias 2017; Pedro 2021). Thus, rock and roll was just another genre that, like so many, was imported from the United States. For example, Bill Haley & His Comets released their single 'Rock Around the Clock' in Spain in 1955 and played in Barcelona in 1958, although the Francoist police dissolved their concert for fear of altercations (Vogel 2017: 198). Another fundamental element to understand the end of Spain's international isolation is tourism, which had become a key productive sector of the national economy and a driver of social change beginning in the late fifties, to the horror of the most conservative elements of the military regime. Some researchers and writers (García Peinazo 2017; Vogel 2017) have pointed out that in 1957, dance orchestras in Spain already included rock and roll, foxtrot, mambo and twist in their repertoire. Since many of these orchestras played for tourists, it was very important to be able to offer a repertoire that included the latest musical novelties to connect with the tastes of an international audience.

Crucially, however, the popularization of rock and roll in Spain had more to do with the impact of certain Latin American bands and Italian and French singers than with Chuck Berry or Buddy Holly. France, Italy and Latin America exported culture and music to Spain: the Italian San Remo festival, the French *chanson*, and styles such as mambo and bolero became very popular there. In the early sixties, Spanish versions of rock and roll hits, like Elvis Presley's 'All Shook Up' (*Estremécete*) and Bill Haley's 'See You Later, Alligator' (*Hasta luego cocodrilo*), by the Cuban band Los Llopis, and of Little Richard's 'Good Golly, Miss Molly' (*La Plaga*), by the Mexican band Los Teen Tops, showed Spanish bands that it was perfectly possible to make rock and roll in Spanish (Pardo 2005). Italian singer Adriano Celentano and Frenchman Johnny Hallyday, who produced music in their own languages, also had an important impact in Spain, serving as examples of how to make rock and roll outside US culture. Therefore, the new rhythms and sounds of rock and roll were disseminated in Spain not only by way of English-speaking countries but also through cultural and linguistic proximities (with Latin European countries and with Latin America, respectively), which were key in these globalization processes.

These exchanges between Spain and Latin America gained new importance in the seventies and eighties, with the arrival in Spain of a number of Argentine musicians who sought refuge from the intensification of the military dictatorship. As Simon Frith (1999) points out, migrations have been one of the most important social changes in the history of popular music. In the case of Spain and Argentina, the arrivals of Xavier Patricio Pérez Álvarez (Gato Pérez), Moris Birabent, the band Aquelarre, Ariel Rot and Alejo Stivel (subsequent members of Tequila) and Andrés Calamaro (in the nineties) were very important for the revitalization of Catalan rumba, singer-songwriters, urban rock and Madrid's new wave. All these musicians brought new ways of doing music that differed from those of Spanish musicians, adapting local themes and sounds from different perspectives without the ideological ties of Spanish cultures. In this way, popular music in Spain could be modernized by breaking the hierarchical model through which musical innovations only emerged from the rock 'metropolises'. For anthropologist Richard M. Shain (2012), when analysing cultural globalization processes, it is important to take into account 'south-south' exchanges, that is, exchanges between countries that are not hegemonic in a given field. As we are seeing, Spanish popular music has been enriched by the contributions, novelties and innovations that came from Argentina, France, Mexico and Italy, just as some Spanish bands have helped to amplify new music scenes in Latin America.[12]

The arrival of foreign musicians in Spain has allowed their Spanish counterparts to contemplate their musical tradition with a different eye and incorporate it into their rock background without prejudice. As musicologist Celsa Alonso (2010) has proposed, based on the work of historian Ismael Saz, Spanish culture and music are largely constructed like a game of mirrors, in which the reflection projected by the gaze of the foreigner (the romantic traveller of the nineteenth century, the American journalist of the seventies, the Argentine musician of the nineties) highlights the value of the music and culture. In a country where cultural and national symbols are continuously discussed (due to their appropriation by the Francoist regime for four decades, and the left's inability to resignify them) and where there is virtually no agreement on the common elements of representation, the external gaze appeases, calms or reinforces: others see what is unique and different about us. In the case of Los Rodríguez, their approach to rumba was, and still is, greatly celebrated by a certain share of music critics. In the context of the nineties, when the indie scene emerged in Spain and rock bands were more focused on imitating English and American rock than on hybridizing it with their national tradition, the vindication of rumba by a group of Argentine artists was very much appreciated, as it was a genre associated with gypsies and the marginalized peripheries of the big cities.

The use of Spanish cultural topics in the lyrics and sound of Los Rodríguez was understood as a slap in the face to the Anglophilia of the bands, audiences and music of the moment. The commemoration in 1992 of the 500th anniversary of the 'discovery' of America, and the transformation of Spain into a cosmopolitan society due to the presence of Latin American and European migrants, forced Spanish society to reconsider its relationships with its former colonies and the bases of its national identity.

The paradox in this case is that the nineties were fruitful years in the hybridization of rumba and flamenco with pop and rock: musicians such as Kiko Veneno, El Último de la Fila, Rosario Flores, Antonio Flores and Manolo Tena topped the charts with albums that were praised by the public, such as *Échate un cantecito* (Sing a Little Song), *De ley* (By Law), *Astronomía razonable* (Reasonable Astronomy) and *Sangre española* (Spanish Blood). However, those albums were not praised by critics in the same way as Los Rodríguez were. Why did critics value the hybridization proposed by Los Rodríguez more than that of Manolo Tena, for example? Was it that music critics valued the foreign gaze more than the native one?

In the following pages, we will try to answer these questions by delving into several issues. First, we offer an analysis of the musical connections between Spain and Latin America, and the important role of Argentine musicians in Spanish popular music. Through this analysis, we will address the various ways in which rock bands in Spain have tried to combine native sounds with foreign inspirations, and how music critics have supported or rejected those hybridizations. We also aim to revisit the Spain of the nineties, describing its political, ideological and aesthetic features as well as its social transformations, to contextualize the musical scenes of that time. Finally, based on these analyses, we will immerse ourselves in the musical legacy of Los Rodríguez and their album *Sin Documentos*, in order to highlight their place in contemporary Spanish culture.

1 Sin Documentos

Musical exchanges between Spain and Latin America

Studies of Spanish and Latin American folk music have developed the concept of *cantes de ida y vuelta*, which literally means 'round-trip songs', to describe folk music forms that emerged in Spain; then travelled to Latin America (due to colonization, migration, slavery or trade); then became adapted to local patterns, features and sounds; and finally travelled back to their place of origin as renewed music forms. As we will see later, rumba is an example of this type of 'round-trip' folk music (Flamencopolis 2021): it resulted from the hybridization of tango flamenco and Cuban *guaguancó*, which together gave rise to Cuban rumba. At the beginning of the twentieth century, these sounds were readapted by flamenco, which led to the birth of flamenco rumba. Then, around 1960, Catalan rumba appeared, led by Peret, with rhythms derived from rumba and rock and roll (Puchades 2011: 56).

The example of rumba serves to illustrate the deep musical connections between Spain and Latin America, which also shaped the national versions of rock and roll, punk, melodic song (or 'light song') and more recently trap and reggaeton. In the case of rock and roll, certain Latin American groups were fundamental for the dissemination of this genre in Spain.[1] They include Los Llopis, a band formed by Cubans who had studied in the United States, which began to make Spanish versions of songs by Bill Haley & His Comets and Elvis Presley. In 1960, Los Llopis played in Spain and recorded some of its popular songs (Domínguez 2002) under the Zafiro record label. Mexican band Los Teen Tops, led by Enrique Guzmán, specialized in Spanish covers of American rock and roll hits and also released its first album in 1960: 'La plaga' was a cover of 'Good Molly Miss Molly', originally recorded by Little Richard (whose hit song 'Tutti Frutti' was also covered in Spanish) while 'El rock de la cárcel' was a cover of Elvis Presley's 'Jailhouse Rock'. The important influence that these bands exerted on Spanish musicians can be perceived in the fact that one of the first hits by Miguel Ríos, an early Spanish rock and roll idol, was a cover of Los Teen Tops' 'Popotitos', which was in turn a Spanish cover of Larry Williams's 'Bony Maronie'.

For the purposes of this book, we will focus some years later, on the seventies and eighties, which saw important arrivals of Argentine musicians, producers and artists in Spain. The military regime that began in Argentina in 1976 forced many citizens into exile in Spain, where the Franco dictatorship had ended just a few months earlier. As Eduardo Viñuela (2019) has pointed out, this migration enriched the Spanish music scenes of that time. For example, Jorge Álvarez, an Argentine record producer and founder of the record label Mandioca, which was key in the awakening of Argentine national rock, came to Spain and worked in the multinational CBS Records, producing successful groups such as Mecano and Olé Olé, the latter of which had an Argentine guitarist, Gustavo Montesano. Moreover, many of the album covers for these groups were created by Argentine designer Juan Gatti. Uruguay also exported notable musicians, such as keyboardist Jorge García Benegas (member of Asfalto) and Hermes Calabria (drummer of Barón Rojo). Spain received talent from Chile as well, like producer Carlos Narea, who worked with top Spanish musicians, and manager Rosa Lagarrigue, who has directed the careers of hugely successful artists such as Miguel Bosé, Mecano and Alejandro Sanz.

Of this group of Latin American musicians, the Spanish music press paid the most attention to Tequila and Moris. Their arrival had an important impact on Spanish popular music as they achieved a very strong connection with the public that only a few contemporary rock bands had managed. A few years later, Los Rodríguez developed their own musical approach by taking advantage of the legacy and open road left by these groups.

The emptiness of Spanish rock

As some journalist and scholars (Manrique and Cuellar 2009; Puchades 2008a; Viñuela 2019) have pointed out, between the late sixties and the beginning of democracy in 1975, Spanish rock lost its momentum, rhythm and capacity to reflect the advances that the genre and Western youth were experiencing hand in hand with counterculture, the hippie movement and progressive rock. The recording industry in Spain did not bet on groups that embodied psychedelia and counterculture, and the Francoist authorities opposed the dissemination of countercultural values. This is what Diego A. Manrique argues, for example, in an article published by the newspaper *El País* to commemorate fifty years of rock in Spain:

> With such impetus, it is surprising that the bands' movement
> disappeared and/or became vulgar in the late sixties. The
> limit of what was possible had been reached: Spanish rock

was not able to keep up with the rhythm set from outside the country, with psychedelia and counterculture. With the scares of 1968 still fresh in memory, the authorities stepped on the brakes: there were times when the appearance of long-haired musicians was forbidden on TVE ….[2] In addition, big record labels did not sympathize with guitarists. In the sixties, many labels were reluctant to allow Spanish groups to record original material and instead privileged Spanish covers of foreign hit songs. (Manrique and Cuellar 2009)

For some Spanish music journalists (Ordovás 1987; Puchades 2008a),[3] this return to the underground slowed down the development of Spanish youth culture, which had begun to emerge with the appearance of the first bands in the sixties, led by Los Bravos and Los Brincos. With the consolidation of democracy and under the influence of punk, rock music achieved cultural notoriety and impact for the first time in Spain, as well as media legitimation, mass appraisal, record-breaking sales and popularity among young people. However, all this occurred belatedly, with the emergence of *La Movida Madrileña* (the Madrid New Wave) (Fouce 2007). For music journalists, the role model was Argentine rock, which became established in those years of standstill in Spain and had the power to create myths, build ties between musicians and fans, produce landmark albums and consolidate the artistic careers of a handful of leading musicians. As Manrique pointed out in another essay:

The Argentine migration [was very important] in the
reinvention of Spanish rock. That republic did not experience
the fracture that sank Spanish rock at the end of the sixties.
On the contrary, the public followed the evolution of

the musicians, and Argentine rock generated a splendid catalogue of creators and developed a peculiar singing style, an artistic universe of its own and a way of facing the world and reflecting its inner reality. (Manrique 1995)

Drawn into the mythification of Argentine rock, Spanish music journalists joyfully welcomed the arrival of some Argentine musicians (mainly Moris, Alejo Stivel and Ariel Rot): the canonical narrative of the history of Spanish rock positions Argentina's contribution to the pop-rock of the Spanish Transition to democracy as decisive for revitalizing the musical scenes, improving the quality of lyrics and melodies and enabling groups to realize that there was a reality of their own to tell in their songs.

According to historians who have worked on Argentine rock (Pujol 2015), its consolidation took place from 1966 to 1973. As mentioned, during this period, Spanish rock was losing the rhythm of musical evolution and began to follow a standardized formula to create commercial songs, which had the support of record companies, such as the so-called Canción del Verano (Summer Hits). In contrast, Argentine rock, baptized as *rock nacional* (national rock) became a key space for the development of youth culture. According to Pujol, the independent record label Mandioca (directed by Jorge Álvarez) played a key role, as it released the first albums by Miguel Abuelo, Manal, Vox Dei and Moris. A little later, other labels released the first records of Sui Generis, Aquelarre and Litto Nebbia. For Pujol, those years witnessed the development of singing and production styles that gradually moved away from the influence of English-speaking countries. Spanish soon became the common language, and musicians developed accents, pronunciations and themes deeply rooted in the Argentine reality. Argentine sociologist Pablo Alabarces (1992) considers the emergence of the band Almendra fundamental to the artistic consolidation of Argentinian rock, due to the lyrics and depth of its songs. In this context, strong and solid connections were built with the youth cultures of the time, and rock became a key element of social identification for young people, beyond political parties and trade unions.

This connection between Argentine rock and youth was further reinforced during the period of military dictatorship (1976–83) (Vila 1985). Although many musicians migrated to flee military violence, rock had a huge boost in those years. The Falklands War generated a paradoxical situation: the military junta banned the broadcasting of English music, which in turn gave national rock the possibility to acquire greater visibility and dissemination, and to become a space of youth resistance against the dictatorship: concerts were filled with anti-dictatorship chants.

As we can see, Argentine rock and Spanish rock took opposite paths of development. In the democratic Argentina of the sixties and seventies, rock became consolidated as a cultural field, capable of building its own spaces and references, away from Anglophone influences. Argentina's national rock created its own idols and lineages, consolidated sites of dissemination and gave rise to an industry that supported the genre. With the arrival of the dictatorship, Argentine rock did not disappear but expanded its links with young people, serving as a space to manifest resistance to the government. In contrast, Spanish rock received little support from record labels, faced the limitations of Franco's censorship and failed to build a strong symbolic space of resistance to Francoism (a space that was occupied by singer-songwriters). As we will see in the subsequent chapters, the musical dynamics of both countries became standardized and aligned in the eighties: the comings and goings of musicians from each side of the Atlantic altered both countries' ways of making rock music.

Tequila and Moris: The myth of Argentine rock

To understand the impact of the arrival of Argentine musicians on Spanish rock scenes during the Transition to democracy, it is necessary to outline what scenes and genres were circulating in Spain in the mid-seventies. As mentioned, between the late sixties and the mid-seventies, rock groups in Spain faced many difficulties to get their albums produced, since the record industry did not pay attention to them. In the mid-seventies, three labels appeared: Zeleste (owned by Edigsa), Gong (owned by Moviplay) and Chapa (owned by Zafiro). These labels began to release rock albums and showcase the variety of styles that existed in Spain in those years. As Domínguez (2004) points out, the main music scenes of the time were Catalan rock (*música laietana*); Andalusian rock and Andalusian gypsy rock; hard rock in Madrid and Castile; and progressive rock in the northwest of the country (García Salueña 2017). Musically, all these scenes fed from progressive rock, symphonic rock and hard rock, mixing these sounds with folk music (flamenco, sardana), native languages (Catalan, Basque, Galician and Asturian) and their own cultural topics (García Peinazo 2017).

In 1976, just a few months after the death of Franco, Ariel Rot arrived in Madrid with his family from Buenos Aires. Rot came from a family with high cultural and social capital. His father, Abrasha Rotenberg, was the editor of the newspaper *La Opinión* and had been threatened by the military junta, which led his family to migrate. His mother, Dina Rot, was a singer and pianist immersed in the cultural and bohemian circles of Buenos Aires, which allowed young Ariel and his sister, renowned actress Cecilia Roth, to meet important musicians, singer-songwriters and artists in their home.

Ariel Rot (Corazón Rural 2018; Puchades 2003) has admitted that, upon his arrival in Spain, his perception of Madrid's rock scenes was not positive. Rot had spent his youth immersed in the key period of consolidation of Argentine rock. In contrast to that rock enculturation, Rot found in Madrid a small rock scene, in which only the venue M&M stood out at all. Rock groups in Madrid imitated to some degree the aesthetics, performances and symbolic universes of American and British rock. Some Spanish groups, like Burning, even sang in English. In Argentina, rock filled stadiums and was a massive cultural product. Argentine musicians like Spinetta and Charly García were stars. Meanwhile in Spain, rock bands faced difficulty getting their music recorded and lacked leaders with mass symbolic capital. Important groups from the previous decade, such as Los Bravos and Los Brincos, split up during this time, and some of their members (such as Juan Pardo) switched to the melodic song genre. Of the pioneers of rock and roll in Spain, only Miguel Ríos, whose 1969 cover version of Ludwig van Beethoven's 'Ode to Joy' had been a huge success, maintained a stable career with links to rock.

After a few months in Madrid, Ariel became a guitarist in the Spoonful Blues Band, which was initially formed by Felipe Lipe and Julián Infante (who later joined Los Rodríguez). The trio was soon joined by Ariel's Argentinian friend Alejo Stivel, whose family was also fleeing the military dictatorship. These four men, plus drummer Manolo Iglesias, later formed Tequila.

Zafiro Records offered the group a recording contract. Initially, Tequila's music was meant to be published by the company's subsidiary record label Chapa, directed by music journalist Vicente Romero, which had specialized in hard rock and urban rock and had already released the first albums of Asfalto, Bloque and Leño. However, executives at Zafiro Records perceived the group's commercial potential. Tequila's rock and roll distanced itself from Madrid's hard rock with a musical approach that was close to the sound of the Rolling Stones and the emerging British New Wave. Tequila's songs were straightforward, infectious and catchy, and its lyrics were youthful and hedonistic: they talked about skipping school and escaping routines, throwing parties and meeting girls. Rock was presented as a release for young people, – nothing that hadn't been sung and told before in other places and languages.

However, in the second half of the seventies, Tequila was a huge novelty in Spain. It recovered the simple and fun rock and roll that Los Llopis and Los Teen Tops had popularized in the sixties. Tequila's catchy melodies contrasted with the seriousness and transcendence of progressive rock, while its hedonism and careless youth stood out against hard rock's vindication of the worker identity. In addition, Tequila offered a carefully crafted image that largely stood out from the rest of the national rock groups. As Ariel Rot has explained, one of the aspects that surprised him the most about the national rock groups was the scant attention they paid to their image (Puchades 2003).

Tequila counterattacked with the help of another expatriate, Juan Gatti,[4] a photographer and designer with experience designing album covers in Argentine rock (for Spinetta, Sui Generis, Claudio Gabis, etc.). Gatti created for Tequila a modern and colourful image, with tight jeans and jackets, which helped the band become popular, appear on the cover of teen magazines and enjoy great success among female listeners. However, Tequila's impact was not limited to public and commercial success. Spanish musicians were also shocked by the appearance of Tequila, by its technical and aesthetic level and its capacity to mobilize youth, far superior to their contemporaries. For Julián Hernández, the drummer of Siniestro Total, Kaka de Luxe (the seminal band of *La Movida Madrileña*) 'looked very seedy next to Tequila. Tequila was the bomb' (Babas and Turrón 2004: 25). It was precisely from the context of Kaka de Luxe and New Wave that some musicians, such as Fernando 'El Zurdo' Márquez (1981), criticized Tequila because, to them, it looked like a 'manufactured' band whose members' families financed its advertising campaign, a point that Rot has denied (Puchades 2003: 71).

Some newspaper articles of the time reflected the fascination that Tequila also generated among certain music journalists, mainly in Madrid. For example, journalist Jesús Ordovás, who was one of the main supporters of the group and had helped them out with their arrival on the Zafiro label, wrote (pseudonymously) in 1978:

> You saw it, man! The other day, there were more girls than boys
> among the ten thousand people that filled the park … it had
> been many, many years since a Spanish group entered that
> list ….[5] How did Tequila manage that, and why didn't Smash,
> Sinum and Máquina? … Perhaps the reason is that all those
> groups were so progressive that they sang in English. … The
> first thing about Tequila that catches people's eyes is how they
> dress. … They take great care of their image, to the point that
> all the money they have must be spent on clothes. (JOB 1978)

On the one hand, we see that language was an important aspect for music critics. Some articles even argued that

Argentine musicians taught their Spanish counterparts to sing in Spanish (Viñuela 2019), though this was certainly an exaggeration, as groups such as Los Canarios and Triana had already released moderately popular rock albums in Spanish. However, it was Tequila who showed that singing in Spanish and making simple and effective rock and roll could grant access to mass audiences. After a few years in which Spanish rock had remained in underground spaces, Tequila brought rock back to commercial success. Several decades later, Los Rodríguez shared with Tequila the ability to connect with audiences who were not interested in rock. Obviously, this generated debates among music critics about the authenticity of the two bands' approaches to music: the eternal dispute between artistic quality and commercial success, between 'selling out' and remaining loyal to a 'distinguished' audience. Nonetheless, the attitude of both groups differed somewhat from that of local Spanish bands. Perhaps what gave Tequila and Los Rodríguez a different perspective was their rock enculturation in Argentina, where, as mentioned, rock constituted a broad community where the debates on art versus commercial music had long been overcome to be able to reach mass audiences.

When assessing Tequila's contributions to Spanish rock culture, it is important to bear in mind, as musicologist Julio Ogas (2019) points out, that migrant musicians must deal with two musical cultures: the origin culture and the destination culture. Musicians develop their own characteristic musical identity within the scenes in which they socialize. However, when they migrate, they must adapt to the receiving culture. In this tension between their own traits and the search for acceptance by the new culture, musicians seek an aesthetic balance in which they lose certain original traits but gain new nuances. In the process, of course, they bring to the host culture a new approach, a different perspective.

In the case of Tequila, the band's main composers, Ariel Rot and Alejo Stivel, had not developed professional careers in Argentina but had been part of the country's rock culture as amateurs. In fact, Tequila's sound and its echoes of classic rock and roll, the Rolling Stones and New Wave had nothing to do with what Argentine rock groups were releasing in the late seventies and early eighties. Tequila's connections with Argentine rock were manifested through the inclusion, on their first two albums, of covers of songs originally performed by Argentine musicians: 'Mr. Jones' by Charly García, 'Las vías del ferrocarril' (Railways) – a cover of 'Trabajando en el ferrocarril' (Working on the Railway) by Pappo's Blues – and 'Rock del ascensor' (Elevator Rock) by the Makaroff brothers. One of the Makaroff brothers, Sergio,[6] also wrote a song for Tequila: 'El ahorcado' (Hanged Man). The songs were not the most iconic within Argentine rock but were the ones that fit perfectly with Tequila's brand of rock and roll.

In turn, as mentioned, Tequila's approach differed from the rest of the urban rock and hard rock groups of the time. In fact, Ariel Rot has shared an anecdote about their clashes with Vicente Romero, director of the Chapa record label and producer of their first album, which reflects the group's character: '[In terms of sound] we tried to stay away from the tacky, distorted and punk guitars he had heard. Because he [Romero] believed that Tequila should have distorted guitars and we did not' (Puchades 2003: 52). Tequila kept its distance from the sound and themes of Madrid rock and became a pioneer in the use of producers outside of Spain (its third and fourth albums were recorded in London) and in self-production (for its second album, together with sound technician Joaquín

Torres). In addition, although Tequila's attitude, aesthetics and lyrics connected it to the emerging Madrid New Wave scene, its instrumental expertise and commercial success did not fit into the punk attitude of some of these groups. A certain connection between Tequila and the rock scenes of that time can be perceived in the instrumental song 'Vacaciones en Copacabana' (Vacations in Copacabana), composed by Rot and the group's drummer, Manolo Iglesias. One might argue that this song could fit with the progressive rock influences of some Spanish bands, albeit filtered through Latin rock and Carlos Santana's guitar. As we will see later, this small sample of hybridization was exploited more clearly by Rot as producer of Andrés Calamaro, and especially as a member of Los Rodríguez.

What seems clear is that Tequila, as would happen later with Los Rodríguez, occupied a space of its own that had similarities with other scenes (urban rock, New Wave) but also clear differences. The members of Tequila have acknowledged that this generated animosity towards them from other contemporary groups, as we have seen, and a lack of support from music journalists, especially when the group began to enjoy commercial success. However, despite its uniqueness, or precisely because of it, Tequila captured the desires of a part of the Spanish youth in a context of cultural effervescence and political change. As journalist César Prieto (in EfeEme 2019) points out, Alejo Sivel and Ariel Rot had lived in an effervescent Buenos Aires, prior to the military junta, so the dynamic Madrid of the late seventies did not surprise them, and they adapted to it with ease.

Tequila's significance to Spanish popular music can be observed, a posteriori, in the groups that, in one way or another, have deepened its musical legacy. This includes Los Rodríguez, as a direct heir, but also Los Ronaldos, Pereza and

El Canto del Loco, which took up the idea of bringing pop and rock to mass audiences, beyond scenes and genres.

Mauricio 'Moris' Birabent (b. 1941, Buenos Aires) is key to assessing the influence of Argentine rock music in Spain and the journalistic discourse around it. Moris, a pioneer of Argentine rock and member of Los Beatniks, immigrated to Spain in the mid-seventies after being designated by the military junta as a musician with subversive ideas (Ogas 2019: 154). Thanks to one of his contacts, Moris got a contract to play in a small pub in Madrid, where a couple of music critics, Jesús Ordovás and Diego A. Manrique, discovered him and were captivated by his style. As these journalists have described (Puchades 2008b), Moris performed only with his electric guitar, with no backing band, combining some songs from his time in Argentina with rock and roll classics and recent compositions in which the city of Madrid was very present.

Like Tequila, Moris received an offer to record with Zafiro's subsidiary label Chapa. His first album, *Fiebre de vivir* (A Fever for Living), was produced by Vicente Romero with Tequila as the backing band. Like Tequila's own music, the 1978 album reclaims a sound linked to classic rock and roll, with straightforward, funny and catchy songs. The first song on the album, 'Sábado a la noche' (Saturday at Night), which includes piano arrangements inspired by Jerry Lee Lewis, engages with the playful and hedonistic spirit of the era that Tequila also captured. The guitars on the album sound quite distorted and somewhat saturated, influenced by the rock sound that Vicente Romero wanted to give to the productions of that time, and which Tequila distanced itself from. The album moves between that distorted rock and instrumental pieces with touches of bossa nova, mid-tempo tracks and two Spanish versions of songs by Carl Perkins and Ray Charles. As for Moris himself, one of the most striking aspects is his voice and his pronunciation. Moris's own aesthetic features are reflected in his Argentine accent, connected with Tango singer, his manner of singing combined with recitations and his powerful voice.

However, what most attracted the attention of music critics were the lyrics written by Moris, who reveals himself as a thorough observer filling his songs with references to the city. What seduced critics is that, as with Tequila, Moris's approach was different from that of other rock groups. As Diego Manrique has explained,

> we did not have anything like him, and on top of that, he knocked us out with a repertoire that mapped the city. Remember that, at that time, our musicians hated their environment: 'Madrid is shit / not even rats can live here'.[7] Imagine the shock: a ragged foreigner who evoked the experiences of the capital's working class ('I am the waiter who serves you beer'). (Manrique 2019: 9)

One of the main features of urban rock was the presence of the city and its neighbourhoods in the lyrics. As Manrique points out, Leño's song denounces the living conditions of the newly built neighbourhoods in the big cities, characterized by its precarious construction, unsanitary conditions and lack of transport. However, Moris's gaze was that of someone who was discovering Madrid and connecting with it, as he himself has pointed out in interviews (Puchades 2007). Songs like 'Balada de Madrid' (Madrid's Ballad) and 'Nocturno de Princesa' (Princess Street at Night) are loaded with references to streets, bars and places in the city. The foreigner's view of Spanish culture, as we have already mentioned, carries enormous weight when it comes to building national and local identity.

For music critics, it was a way to reconnect with a city that was changing and evolving. Moreover, the tone that Moris used in his songs was also uncommon among national rock groups: it is a costumbrist tone that narrates urban scenes that have no great significance but that add depth to the songs and locate them in a specific time and place. In an interview conducted at the time, Moris expressed his surprise at the poor ability of rock groups to observe their environment:

> Compared to Argentina, I think it [Spanish rock] is a little more distanced from ordinary people's feelings, from their intimate issues. There is no training to assess reality. I believe that, at some point, people here will discover all the value of the Spanish world, the value of this glass of cognac at three in the afternoon … the Casa de Campo.[8] (Arnáiz 1978)

Moris perceived something that, years later, Andrés Calamaro would also portray in his songs: the value of everyday life in Spanish culture. Costumbrism also featured in another scene of great importance in those years in Spain: that of singer-songwriters, which developed in Spain primarily during the Franco regime and became a key element in the cultural resistance to the dictatorship. In addition to political speech, singer-songwriters developed a poetic discourse. This genre musicalized such poets as Antonio Machado, Federico García Lorca and Miguel Hernández, drawing on these poets' use of costumbrism to bring their songs closer to the people. From that perspective, the emergence of Moris united two worlds that had been far apart until then: rock and the singer-songwriter genre. In fact, Joaquín Sabina, whose career developed between the two scenes, acknowledged in one of his biographies that Moris was one of his inspirations to move between those worlds (Sabina and Menéndez Flóres 2008: 85).

Following the approach of Julio Ogas (2019) on migrant musicians, already discussed in the case of Tequila, Ogas identifies two key moments in Moris's career in Spain. The first one is his debut album, in which he keeps using some of the forms already present in his work in Argentina but gradually adapts them to the new environment: the influence of tango and other Latin music genres, his taste for ballads and classic rock and roll and the use of the city and specific locations. On this album, Moris also began to use Spanish jargon, like *metro*, *tia* (chick) and *chaval* (lad), reflecting the assimilation of his new reality. In subsequent albums, such as *Mundo Moderno* (Modern World) (1980), Moris pushed rock and roll aside to give way to sounds closer to New Wave – which in the eighties had a great influence on pop and rock – while maintaining his eclecticism.

As with Tequila, Moris's contribution has been highly valued by Spanish music critics, both for his use of Spanish in a somewhat Anglophile context and for placing Madrid, its streets and its people at the centre of his songs. Moris also occupied a space of his own in the rock ecosystem of the seventies and eighties. In his case, alternating between classic rock and roll, ballads, Latin music and a singer-songwriter style, he paved the way for Joaquín Sabina, Enrique Urquijo, Quique González and, as we will see later, Andrés Calamaro, one of the frontmen of Los Rodríguez.

The fame and recognition of Moris and Tequila in Spain was intense yet brief, with both their careers becoming overshadowed in the early eighties. Tequila disbanded in 1982[9] due to a fall in album sales, drug addictions, internal problems and legal issues with the label. For his part, Moris did not enjoy the same reception in Spain after his first album. Becoming increasingly disenchanted with his host country, he prepared to return to Argentina (Puchades 2007). However, in 1982, Miguel Ríos released the live album *Rock & Ríos*, which was followed by an extensive and well-prepared tour with enormous public and sales success. The album was released at a time of great polarization in the field of pop-rock as it competed against the hard and heavy rock groups of La Movida bands (Val Ripollés 2017), which were influenced by New Wave, punk and techno. As previously explained, Miguel Ríos was one of the few pioneers of rock and roll in Spain who had remained active. At the end of the seventies, this musician from Granada had redirected his sound towards rock, and this live album was perceived as his endorsement of the rock scene. On the live album, Miguel Ríos included covers of several Madrilenian rock groups (Burning, Leño, Topo), Tequila ('Rock and roll en la plaza del pueblo' / 'Rock and Roll in the Town Square') and Moris ('Sábado a la noche' / 'Saturday at Night'). Symbolically, Ríos deemed Tequila and Moris as key artists in the rebirth of the genre during the Spanish Transition to democracy and canonized them alongside other important bands of that era. As Moris himself has acknowledged (Puchades 2007), that recognition helped him further consolidate his career in Spain.

The massive success of Tequila, which appealed to the rock tradition, and Moris's work as a bridge between singer-songwriters and rockers are fundamental elements for understanding the connection that was established between Argentine national rock and Spanish rock, which began to consolidate into a new identity after Franco's dictatorship. The reception of their songs by music critics also allows us to capture the process of canonization of Argentine rock as a role model for Spaniards. In both cases, these situations reappeared a decade later when the massive success of Los Rodríguez and the idolization of Andrés Calamaro forced the Spanish public and critics to think once again about the role of Argentine musicians in the national rock scene.

2   Mi Rock Perdido

The production context of *Sin Documentos*

The Spain to which Rot returned in 1990 to form Los Rodríguez was very different from the one that had brought about the success of Tequila. As globalization was advancing, Spain had consolidated its democracy and joined the European Union. The Spanish economy was increasingly connected to international trends, and the lifestyle of Spanish citizens was increasingly cosmopolitan. In this context, the Spanish cultural and musical traditions were being redefined after the eighties, a decade in which popular music had played an unusual role in defining the external image of Spain and the national identity of its citizens.

In Spain's recent history, the improvement of living conditions has always been linked to greater openness to the outside world. In the sixties, the signing of agreements with the United States and the arrival of tourists put an end to two decades of isolation caused by the dictatorship. In 1985, with the Spanish Socialist Party (*Partido Socialista Obrero Español*, PSOE) in government, Spain acceded to the European Economic Community. The eighties were a time of enormous economic adjustments and immense unemployment (especially among young people). 'This modernization involved unavoidable sacrifices that in the medium term would allow [Spain] to enjoy the prosperity of its northern neighbours' (González Férriz 2020: 53). The unrest and social protests of the late eighties forced the socialist government to change its policy: the budget for 1990 and 1991 increased social spending and public investments, including those linked to 'two events whose explicit purpose was to show the world that Spain had entered modernity' (55). In 1992, the year of the signing of the Maastricht Treaty, which granted freedom of movement and residence for persons in the European Union (EU), Spain hosted the Olympic Games in Barcelona and the Universal Exhibition in Seville.

The latter event, Expo '92, was a celebration of the 500th anniversary of Columbus's journey to the Americas, the 'Age of Discovery'. In the words of King Juan Carlos I, the objective of Expo '92 was to celebrate 'dialogue between peoples, mutual knowledge, cultural exchange and shared information, as ways of understanding and solidarity' (González Férriz 2020: 55). In this event, Spain uncritically vindicated its relationship with Latin American countries, which led to faint criticism of its inability to recognize the colonial character of this relationship (Roa Bastos 1991).

Both events were attended by delegates from all countries and involved huge investments in both cities. Spain opened its first high-speed train line, between Madrid and Seville; redeveloped an abandoned part of Seville (Isla de la Cartuja in the Guadalquivir River, headquarters of the Expo); and built new hotels and highways. An important part of Barcelona was reorganized to open the city to the sea and modernize it, which in the following years made it one of the most visited European cities.[1]

This 'collective madness' was born in a moment of national 'economic euphoria' (González Férriz 2020: 59) and a complicated international economic context. The 1990–1 Gulf War had pushed up the price of oil. The bursting of Japan's asset price bubble in 1990 weakened its economy and strained the international currency market. In 1992, the same year as the Expo '92 and the Barcelona Olympics, a collapse in the pound sterling forced the United Kingdom to withdraw from the European Exchange Rate Mechanism. The massive public investments prior to the events of 1992 delayed the arrival of the crisis in Spain, but after that year, it became the European country with the most job losses and the largest decrease in gross domestic product (GDP) (77). In the following years, Spain's national currency, the peseta, was devalued several times. The crisis was brief yet intense: in 1995 the Spanish economy entered a long expansionary cycle, fuelled by easy credit and real estate speculation, which left the country particularly weak to face the next great global crisis of 2008.

The economic crisis of the nineties occurred after the fall of the Berlin Wall that came to legitimize neoliberal economic globalization, which in turn became a highly contested political concept (as proven by the protests and riots against the World Trade Organization in Seattle in 1999 and in Genoa in 2011). Unrest slowly gestated and erupted at the end of this decade – the decade in which Los Rodríguez developed their musical production. Argentina, the home country of Rot and Calamaro, was one of the countries that suffered the most from the adjustments of the international financial economy.

In 1999, the government of Raúl Alfonsín, the first democratic president after the military dictatorship, decreed the devaluation of the Argentine austral: almost half of all Argentines dropped below the poverty line because their wages did not allow them to buy food, which resulted in looting and rioting in the main cities. This economic 'debacle', represented by crowds looting supermarkets in search of food (Osvaldo Esteban 2015: 127), pushed those with the possibility of buying a plane ticket to migrate. Spain (along with Italy) was one of the European countries that welcomed more Argentines. 'In 1989 Spain was a spectacular celebration, while Argentina was stuck in terrible inflation, with shortages' (Babas and Turrón 2020: 24). While the parents of Ariel Rot and Alejo Stivel had arrived in Madrid in the seventies fleeing military repression, Rot returned to Madrid in 1990 pushed by hyperinflation, in a context in which 'emigrating ceased to be a sign of individualism to become a collective behaviour' (Mira 2005: 131).

Spain's relationship with migration also changed between Ariel Rot's two trips. In 1985, the country recorded for the first time more inflows than outflows of migrants: after decades of exporting cheap labour to France, Switzerland and Germany and sending its young people to venture out to Cuba or Argentina, growing economic prosperity was turning Spain into a land of opportunity. The nineties began an important transformation of Spanish society with the progressive arrival of immigrants, especially from Latin American countries and Morocco. In 1991, a total of 360,000 immigrants settled in the country, with the annual number rising to 637,000 in 1998. As a percentage of the population, immigrants rose from 0.9 per cent at the beginning of the decade to 2.3 per cent in 2000, continuing to grow in parallel with the economic take-off of the country, which needed labour in the service and agriculture sectors. In the new century, Spain experienced one of the highest annual immigration rates in the world. Currently, 11 per cent of the Spanish population is of immigrant origin (I.N.E. 2020).

This increase in immigration that began slowly but steadily in the nineties was transforming Spanish cities into more cosmopolitan and global places. At the same time, rejection of foreigners grew, and xenophobic incidents multiplied. Newspapers of the nineties covered the numerous aggressions promoted by racist skinheads, who soon began to confront other subcultures (Martínez Arhens 1995).

In November 1992, a Dominican woman, Lucrecia Pérez, was murdered in the Madrid neighbourhood of Aravaca. Gatherings of Dominican immigrants in a public park had led to arguments with neighbours and even some confrontations with police. In this climate of tension, on the night of 13 November, four masked young men entered the abandoned Four Roses nightclub, which was squatted by Dominican immigrants, and fired shots, killing Pérez on the spot. These right-wing extremists were arrested and tried, which gave visibility to the existence of organized xenophobic groups.

In 2000, in El Ejido, a southern Spanish town with a large population of sub-Saharan immigrants who pick fruit and vegetables in vast greenhouses, a crowd enraged by the murder of a local young woman at the hands of a young African man with mental problems destroyed the places where the immigrant workers lived (Constenla 2000). For several days, more than six hundred policemen clashed with these local citizens until normalcy was restored. As writer Juan Goytisolo (Bermúdez 2018: 112) explained, racism is the negative effect of economic growth.

Popular music: Tradition and cosmopolitanism

The Spain of the nineties was therefore a space of transformation and conflict from which popular music could not escape. In the musical field, the tension between tradition and modernity translated into the clash between nationalism and cosmopolitanism. With the transformation of Spanish society into a multicultural society, the nineties are a hinge between a Spain inherited from Francoism and a Spain that has joined the flows of globalization.

During the eighties, the national version of the New Wave developed in Spain under the name of *La Movida Madrileña*. It was a movement that shared the immediacy and rupturism of punk in a very different context: in the eighties the Spanish Transition to democracy was consolidated, especially after the electoral victory of the PSOE in 1982. Young Spaniards also suffered from the oil crisis; however, their disenchantment was caused not by dissatisfaction with the post-war consensus but by the rejection of both the heritage of Francoism and anti-Franco militancy. The punk rejection of the virtuosity of symphonic rock was parallel to the rejection of the music of the politicized singer-songwriters of the seventies. Young people in *La Movida Madrileña* were urban, modern and hedonistic; they rejected the political struggle and took to the streets to the rhythm of short songs. The new democratic governments appropriated the vitality of the youth movement to win the vote of the youngest population and to offer an image of a modern and dynamic country that had left the dictatorship behind. *La Movida Madrileña* 'became a showcase for the country's (post-)modernity and new democratic credentials both at home and abroad' (Wheeler 2016: 144).

Spanish groups from the eighties were influenced by their contemporary counterparts from London and New York and by the punk, mod and post-punk subcultures. The most important difference was that Spanish bands from the eighties sang in Spanish, whereas some Spanish rock groups from previous decades had used English as a starting point: as we have seen, Tequila, the first Spanish group formed by Ariel Rot and Julián Infante, was in this sense ahead of its time under the influence of Argentine rock.

La Movida Madrileña developed a contradictory relationship with the Spanish musical tradition: in the early years, Spanish bands mimicked their English and American counterparts and only resorted to Spanish genres, such as *copla*,[2] with a camp attitude, 'as a way for connoisseurs to celebrate the alienation, distance and incongruity of the values on which the taste of the moment was built' (Fouce and Pecourt 2008). A paradigmatic example is the scene in the film *What Have I Done to Deserve This?* (1984), in which film director Pedro Almodóvar himself appears in a television programme, dressed as a Napoleonic soldier and singing the well-known copla 'La bien pagá' (A Well-Paid Woman) to transvestite artist Fabio McNamara.

As the decade progressed, certain sounds and references to Spanish culture were reclaimed without irony or distance: in 1984 Gabinete Caligari included on its first album the songs 'Que Dios reparta suerte' (May God Spread Good Luck) and 'Sangre española' (Spanish Blood). Both songs are set in the world of bullfighting and incorporate popular expressions ('Que Dios reparta suerte' is the motto bullfighters repeat before going out to the ring) as well as nods to Spanish folklore, such as the use of castanets and *pasodoble*, the music genre most linked to the world of bullfighting. In 1985, Radio Futura, the most popular group of the moment, released a different version of its song 'Semilla negra' (Black Seed) with the collaboration of flamenco guitarist Raimundo Amador. For Silvia Bermúdez (2018: 29), this remix is an 'attempt at musical hybridization' that is pushed further in a new version in 1992, with Latin arrangements in winds and percussion, showing that 'musicians from the Movida period have much to learn from … *soneros* about rhythm in speech, sound, and motion' (43). On that same remix album, *Tierra para bailar* (Earth to Dance), the group revisited another one of its songs, 'Paseo con la negra flor' (A Walk with the Black Flower), intensifying its rumba heritage.

The year 1992 can be considered the definitive extinction of *La Movida Madrileña*, although some groups are still active. For authors such as Teresa Vilarós (1998), this year marks the end of the Transition to democracy. According to González Férriz, 1992 witnessed 'the renovation of a popular culture that so far had been dominated, thematically and generationally, by the great contemporary cultural movement of the Transition: *La Movida Madrileña*' (2020: 63). Four unknown groups, signed by the small label *Elefant*, organized a small national tour called 'Noise Pop 92', exhibiting the incipient indie scene that was appearing in Spain. *La Movida Madrileña* 'had lost all its provocative and transgressive power' (63), and a new generation was beginning to create its own spaces.

However, the first musicians with whom the members of Los Rodríguez interacted upon arriving in Spain came out of *La Movida Madrileña*. The Spanish-Argentine band spent long hours in the rehearsal rooms of Tablada Street,[3] where Madrid's rock elite (Pistones, Los Ronaldos and Gabinete Caligari) also used to rehearse. Los Rodríguez gained prestige and respect among their colleagues thanks to their work ethic. Germán Vilella, the drummer of the group, has mentioned that 'even in the wildest times', he never broke the habit of 'going to play and rehearse alone'.[4] Los Rodríguez participated in jam sessions to stay active. When they started performing live, they filmed each concert to analyse their performance afterwards. 'From Siroco to Las Ventas',[5] they repeat in their 1993 performance opening for Manolo Tena at the Las Ventas bullfighting ring, which was commercially released in 2020. As a kind of meritocratic mantra, Los Rodríguez remarked that, to achieve success and get to play in bullfighting rings, they first had to play at clubs, bars and small venues, sometimes with a small audience. This statement reflects a key ideological element of rock: the Calvinist work ethic, in which work always requires effort and carries a reward. Rock groups would differ from pop groups in the sense that the success of the former would be a product of hard work, effort, years of hardship and intense touring (Keightley 2006), with the only payoff being, perhaps, a certain prestige.

Although Los Rodríguez interacted with the rock bands of the time, its musical approach did not fit with them. Proof of this is the set that Los Rodríguez performed in their first rehearsal (according to Babas and Turrón 2020: 40), which included 'Princesa' (Princess) by Joaquín Sabina. This song shows the connections between Sabina and the Spanish-Argentine group, whose three surviving members (Rot, Calamaro and Vilella) symbolically re-recorded it in 2020 on a tribute album to the musician. The rock scenes that developed in Spain in the late 1980s and early 1990s moved between political rock, linked to punk, in the case of urban rock (Extremoduro, Reincidentes); an incipient noise rock, in which some Spanish groups sang in English, which was later reflected in indie (El Inquilino Comunista, Los Planetas); some successful groups that came from the previous decade, linked to *La Movida Madrileña* (Gabinete Caligari, La Frontera, Los Ronaldos); and an emerging garage rock and punk scene located in Madrid's Malasaña area, with Spanish bands that write their songs in English (Pleasure Fuckers, Sex Museum). The aesthetics of Los Rodríguez did not end up fitting into any of those scenes, which is similar to what happened with Tequila in the seventies. In terms of lyrics or sound, Los Rodríguez resembled neither urban rock nor the garage scenes: the group was not inspired by punk or hard rock genres, nor did its lyrics concern political issues. In the case of indie, Los Rodríguez were from another generational era, showed no musical interest in noise or grunge and did not write music in English. There were more musical links with the rock bands from Madrid, like Los Ronaldos (via the Rolling Stones) and, above all, Gabinete Caligari (via hybridization), although the lyrics of Los Rodríguez were often focused on emotions, which separated them from those groups.

Gabinete Caligari was one of the most seasoned of the Tablada Street bands. Veterans of *La Movida Madrileña*, this band transitioned from post-punk into pop with resonances of Spanish popular culture. Its breakout album was *Camino Soria* (On the Way to Soria) (EMI 1987), which quoted classical Spanish poets such as Gustavo Adolfo Bécquer and Antonio Machado, who had written verses set in the Castilian city. Earlier, with 'Al calor del amor en un bar' (In the Heat of Love in a Bar) (DRO/Tres Cipreses 1986), Gabinete Caligari reconstructed a scene in a popular bar including street slang. The group's singer, Jaime Urrutia, introduced Calamaro to the world of bullfighting and took him to the Las Ventas bullfighting ring for the first time.

Urrutia and his popular tastes had a very strong influence on Calamaro.[6] Calamaro was very clear from the beginning of his Spanish stage that he had to incorporate popular elements in order to capture the masses and appeal to the crowds that filled the summer festivals and *verbenas*, not only to rock connoisseurs, even if it meant setting aside some elements of his Argentine background. As Ariel Rot narrates, 'we wanted to be a group from here, from Madrid. We knew that Argentine groups fail when they come to Spain. … We had to investigate Spain and then return' (Babas and Turrón 2020: 172).

As mentioned, one of the first songs that Los Rodríguez performed in that initial rehearsal was 'Princesa' by Joaquín Sabina, who shared with them an interest in popular issues and stories of mischief-makers and party animals. Sabina had started his musical career within the group of anti-Franco singer-songwriters, but throughout the eighties his albums drifted towards more of a rock sound with the collaboration of guitarist Pancho Varona. Sabina was an heir of the tradition of urban bards, which includes Moris. Sabina's songs also contained many references to the city's streets, sites and hallmarks. In fact, one of Sabina's most famous songs is titled 'Pongamos que hablo de Madrid' (Let's Say I'm Talking about Madrid). Within the rock scene, Sabina was not well regarded, so he publicly recognized the respect that Los Rodríguez had shown to him. The connection between Los Rodríguez and Sabina is also based on the fact that, just like Calamaro and Rot, Sabina introduced in his lyrics emotional and relationship issues from the perspective of the heterosexual male, leaving aside the political topics that had characterized singer-songwriters in the Transition.

Musically, Sabina had been approaching popular Latino music genres (*ranchera*, *bolero*) since the eighties, combining them with more of a rock sound and echoes of the Rolling Stones, J. J. Cale and Bob Dylan, all influences shared by Los Rodríguez. It is worth noting that on their final tour in 1996, Los Rodríguez opened for Sabina. Therefore, the version of Sabina's song that Los Rodríguez performed in its first rehearsal anticipated that the group was going to occupy a space of its own, more related to singer-songwriters than to rock groups. This allowed Los Rodríguez to take certain liberties in their compositions, bringing a different perspective to Spanish pop-rock that was uniquely theirs.

The rest of the songs performed in that first rehearsal also give us clues about the group's identity. Los Rodríguez covered songs originally performed by Tequila, the Rolling Stones, Charly García and Los Abuelos de la Nada ('Mil horas'). The inclusion of Tequila's songs is not surprising, given that Ariel Rot and Julián Infante had previously been in that group. In fact, in their early years Los Rodríguez introduced themselves as a band of former Tequila members, which was not a very fruitful tactic. As David Bonilla[7] recalls:

> Tequila was quite forgotten in Spain. For many years, the memory of Tequila was a bit hidden. As a teenager I remembered them, their pictures and clothes and listening to them on the radio, but then there is just a void. Many people completely forgot about Tequila, and Los Rodríguez reminded them that they had existed.[8] (Personal communication, 29 September 2019, Madrid)

As we will see, Los Rodríguez gradually transitioned from being identified with Tequila to having a name of their own, although in Argentina the band was more recognized thanks to Andrés Calamaro. However, the association of Los Rodríguez with Tequila caused some record labels to see the former as an outdated project, formed by musicians who had already burnt through their chance at Spanish rock.

As for the rest of the cover songs, we have already commented on the influence of the Rolling Stones on the sound of Los Rodríguez (and even on the appearance of Julián Infante, similar to that of Keith Richards). The quota of 'Argentineness' was met by covering Charly García, which

Tequila had also done, and 'Mil horas' (A Thousand Hours), a classic 'rock nacional' anthem composed by Andrés Calamaro while he was a member of Los Abuelos de la Nada, although it was not as popular in Los Rodríguez repertoire.

However, despite the popular success of Gabinete Caligari and Joaquín Sabina, critics' attention in the nineties was focused on the emergence of indie after the Noise Pop tour. The bands born in the indie scene were the antithesis of Los Rodríguez, having neither an interest in Spanish popular culture nor ties with Latin America. These groups sang in English and were influenced by Nirvana, Sonic Youth and Dinosaur Jr. Los Planetas was the only group of the first batch that opted to sing in Spanish (and the one that has had the longest journey, still active even today), but their noisy aesthetic buried their voices with guitars. Over time, the indie scene became populated with groups that sang in Spanish, and even Los Planetas incorporated flamenco sounds. However, the young generation of the nineties had their eyes and ears focused on music sung in English. Even though Indie music achieved a lot of media visibility in the nineties, it possibly never corresponded with its massive success: this was achieved later with the emergence of Spanish-singing bands such as Love of Lesbian, Izal and Vetusta Morla, in the 2010s.

It was at the nineties that the summer festival scene was born. At the end of the crisis of 1993, municipalities were able to collect money from building licences once again and started to launch promotional campaigns in order to attract high-spending tourists and create a modern image for the city. However, this scene was built in the early years of the decade by small independent labels, festivals and media outlets that gave legitimacy to the movement. Established music critics celebrated the emergence of the indie scene, largely due to the high cultural capital of the groups, which the journalists themselves shared: 'journalists are like most members of the groups, middle-class, college students. … Those who have taken over the media have the same tastes as the bands and have helped to hype this scene' (González Férriz 2020: 148).

However, the appearance of Los Rodríguez, the success of *Sin Documentos* in 1993 and the bet they placed on Spanish rhythms were not an isolated event in Spanish music. In the early nineties, several new pop-rock albums were noticeably influenced by rumba and achieved remarkable sales success. In 1991, Seguridad Social, a band that had started playing punk, released *Chiquilla*, and the next year, Manolo Tena (who had found some success in the previous decade with his band Alarma) released *Sangre española* (Sony 1992). In a promotional interview, Tena stated that the album had come out 'at the right time, when the public's taste was right for these songs' (Íñiguez 1993). After playing blues and rock in the underground scene, he succeeded with an album based on rumba rhythms, Spanish guitar sounds and castanets. The chorus of his first single speaks of 'gypsy passion and Spanish blood, when I'm with you alone'. There was no place for rock purism: 'The good thing about the nineties is that we are all much more eclectic than before. Anything can sell, be it ethnic music, rock, funk, salsa, ballad or *bakalao* [Spanish techno music]' (Íñiguez 1993).

In 1992, Kiko Veneno, who was the father of gypsy rock in the seventies with his group Veneno, and had composed some of the hits of flamenco legend Camarón de la Isla, recorded *Échate un cantecito* (Sing a Little Song). This album has become a classic of Spanish pop. Music critic Diego Manrique recalls that Kiko Veneno 'had fifteen years of great ideas … that always remained in the underground. … After noticing that his lyrics did not communicate, he discovered the intelligibility model of the carnival groups of Cádiz' (2000). In the same way as Los Rodríguez, the use of rumba and references to national popular culture catapulted the album to fame. And in parallel to the group formed by Rot and Calamaro, Kiko Veneno turned to a non-Spanish producer, the British Jo Dworniak, 'who covered his songs with slender flesh' (Manrique 2000) and had already worked with Radio Futura on their journey to a more Latin sound in the previous decade.

It is also important to note that there was a noticeable distance between critics' tastes and the reality of music consumption in the country. In the nineties, when Alejandro Sanz consolidated his career as a mass idol, he reclaimed the ballad tradition of Julio Iglesias but also incorporated his background in flamenco. Indeed, his 1997 hit song 'Corazón partío' (Broken Heart) is also a rumba.

Rosario Flores released her successful album *De ley* that same year. She was the daughter of two flamenco artists, singer Lola Flores and guitarist Antonio 'El Pescailla', known for his style of playing rumbas. In 2016, indie magazine *Jenesaispop* published a song-by-song review of the album; the author, well-known producer Guille Mostaza, called the album a 'masterpiece of the national mainstream' and 'a perfect fusion between her parents' generation and her own' (Mostaza 2016).

Many of the songs on Flores's album were composed by her brother Antonio Flores, who was part of Los Rodríguez's inner circle. Rot referred to Antonio as 'another member of Los Rodríguez', and Calamaro recalled, 'We were friends. We tried to learn the rhythm of flamenco songs. … He came a lot to [our house on] Martínez Campos [Street]. … He used to take us to see live music shows, and we got along very well' (Babas and Turrón 2020: 60). This friendship led to the collaboration in which Antonio Flores recorded the song 'Engánchate conmigo' (Hook Up with Me) for the band's 1992 album *Disco pirata*. This song with its rumba influences anticipated some of the elements, particularly the use of percussion, that would appear later in the single 'Sin Documentos' which catapulted Los Rodríguez to fame.

3 Pequeño Salto Mortal

How the music of Los Rodríguez fascinated Spain

Los Rodríguez's musical career was short but prolific: just six years of recording history (1991–6) in which they produced five albums. As David Bonilla explains, 'The life of Los Rodríguez was very brief and intense. They had all the ingredients: failure, success, drugs and death; and all the myths of rock documentaries' (personal communication, 29 September 2019, Madrid). Another element, another rock cliché, can be added to the history of Los Rodríguez: their rise to success, from playing in bars and halls to finishing their career touring with Joaquín Sabina and selling out bullfighting arenas. We have already commented on the importance of the phrase 'From Siroco to Las Ventas' in the group's career, and their vindication of their work ethic and effort. Despite the hardships, disagreements and albums that did not obtain success they desired at first, Los Rodríguez soon managed to earn the respect of contemporary bands. According to the logic of rock authenticity (Keightley 2006), bands that get success quickly are perceived with certain distrust (as in the case of Tequila), while bands that succeed after overcoming difficulties are regarded as authentic. From this perspective, it looks like Los Rodríguez achieved rock authenticity.

The album that changed the course of Los Rodríguez was *Sin Documentos*. Released in 1993, the album allowed the group to leave the rock halls and reach the so-called general public: playing on radio stations, performing at local festivals and becoming known beyond the realm of music criticism. *Sin Documentos* is not Los Rodríguez's best-selling album – that honour goes to the compilation they released before splitting up (*Hasta luego*) – but its hit title track, combining rumba and rockabilly on a catchy riff, became embedded in Spanish musical memory. As we will see below, *Sin Documentos* was a difficult album to make: no record label showed interest in publishing it over the course of a year, which generated uncertainties and tensions within the band, such that Andrés Calamaro envisioned a prolific future alone. The relative commercial success of the album only increased those tensions, which would be palpable in the recording of the next album, *Palabras más, palabras menos* (1995). *Sin Documentos*, in hindsight, could be seen as the beginning of the end for the band.

So, then, where did Los Rodríguez begin? We can locate the beginning in several peer relationships that developed over time. We have already described the first one: the friendship between Ariel Rot and Julián Infante, the guitarists of Tequila. After the group split up, both continued to collaborate professionally in Rot's solo career, as well as in the production and recording of other Spanish groups, such as the 1983 album *Persecución* by Pistones. As previously discussed, Rot decided to return to his native Argentina in the mid-eighties, where he met Andrés Calamaro, who had a similar musical past (both were members of successful bands, such as Tequila and Los

Abuelos de la Nada) but an uneven solo career. Calamaro began to work and perform together with Rot, who helped him produce two solo records. This became the second key relationship.

The third and most decisive relationship for the formation of Los Rodríguez is the meeting between drummer Germán Vilella and Julián Infante. As we have seen, Infante remained active after the separation of Tequila, collaborating with Ariel Rot until the mid-eighties and performing with successful groups such as Glutamato Ye-Yé, Desperados and Pistones. For his part, Vilella[1] was a drummer with considerable experience in various scenes: he had played with heavy metal groups, pop groups (Álex & Christina, Mercedes Ferrer), rock groups (Luz Casal) and singer-songwriters (Luis Eduardo Aute), and he had a relationship with flamenco musicians, from Ketama to Antonio Flores. In the San Blas district, on the periphery of Madrid, Vilella met and befriended Julián Infante, and they began to plan joint projects.

One of those projects was to form a group with singer Fernando de Diego. In the process, the first pairing came back into contact: in the summer of 1990, Infante invited Rot to a Rolling Stones concert in Madrid. Rot accepted this transoceanic invitation and was dazzled by Madrid's music scene. Although he had barely been away for four years, he noticed that the technical equipment, ticket prices, audiences and working conditions of rock groups had markedly improved, while in Argentina the economic and social situation had worsened, with hyperinflation and power cuts. As we have seen, the nineties in Spain were perceived as a continuation of the eighties, a time of economic prosperity in which consumerism entered Spanish society with force. Ariel Rot points out that 'there is talk of the eighties, but the Madrid of the early nineties was spectacular: many places, many things, many stages, people on the street and money in their pockets' (Babas and Turrón 2020: 24). In the words of Germán Vilella: 'in the nineties, there was a lot of joy, everything was carefree. People didn't care about animal abuse, politics, the Iraq war or anything. People were dedicated to living' (personal communication, 15 June 2019, Figueras).

The Rot–Calamaro partnership (1988–90)

In Chapter 2, we reviewed the musical and social contexts in which Los Rodríguez developed their career. However, to understand the band's origins and development, it is important to analyse the creative relationship established between Ariel Rot and Andrés Calamaro prior to Los Rodríguez, because it defined the sonic and aesthetic foundations that continued later in the Hispanic-Argentine band. After the dissolution of Tequila, Rot released two albums with Zafiro Records in 1984 and 1985: *Debajo del puente* (Under the Bridge) and *Vértigo*. These albums, with a darker sound and lyrics than Tequila's music, had little success among the Spanish public but were received with interest in Argentina, which in turn made Rot consider working as producer for Soda Stereo, one of the most successful Argentine bands of the moment: 'modernity reached Buenos Aires and I became the most modern arrival from Spain … we arrived in Buenos Aires and it was like the beginning of the eighties there' (quoted in Puchades 2003: 117). According to Argentine researcher Cristian Secul Giusti (2016), in the eighties, once the military dictatorship had ended and Raúl Alfonsín came into power in 1983, Argentine rock lost the solemnity of previous decades and became more ironic and hedonistic, similarly to Spanish pop-rock in the same decade. Popular music opened up to the exploration of emotional and sexual themes and addressed issues concerning desire, dance and eroticism.

> The spaces were first occupied by pop bands with fun aesthetics (Los Abuelos de la Nada, Los Twist, Las Viudas e Hijas de Rock and Roll, produced by Charly García) and by the 'modern' bands which claimed the physical dimension and dance as elements traditionally ignored by mainstream national rock (Virus, Soda Stereo, Zas). (Semán and Vila, quoted in Secul Giusti 2016: 99)

It is in one of these very bands, Los Abuelos de la Nada, that Andrés Calamaro stood out as keyboardist. By the end of the seventies, Calamaro had already developed professional experience with the candombe-rock band Raíces as well as with Los Abuelos de la Nada, with whom he had written the hit song 'Mil horas' in 1983. However, the solo career he started in the mid-eighties did not end up bearing fruit. Even so, in this new generation of bands and composers, such as Fito Páez and Gustavo Cerati, Calamaro stood out for his lyrics:

> As an author and creator of famous Argentine rock songs, Calamaro has been able to generate a poetic repertoire full of quests, experiences and reflections linked to love, music, vice, society and freedom, which made him stand out as an artist of the counterculture. (Mascia, quoted in Secul Giusti 2016: 213)

Love and heartbreak are common topics in popular music, albeit more prominent in some scenes and genres than in others. As

Carolina Abello (2018) points out, love has been a constant theme in Argentine rock lyrics, but it has been depicted from a heterosexual male perspective, in which women are treated only as objects of male desire. We can therefore understand that Calamaro continued a trend started by such artists as Charly García and Luis Alberto Spinetta, but also revitalized these topics with new sounds and aesthetics. We cannot dismiss the impact that tango could have had on all these songwriters. Love songs, centred on men being disappointed and suffering from betrayal, are a constant of the symbolic universe of tango. Ariel Rot also explored emotional issues in some of the songs on his solo albums, such as 'Sin saber qué decir' (Not Knowing What to Say). The interesting thing about this issue is that when Calamaro arrived in Spain with that lyrical background, he offered a different perspective to that of the native rock scenes. Heartbreak and the idea of the *femme fatale* had worked as topics in some music scenes of the eighties, such as heavy metal, but broadly speaking, Spanish rock had not focused on those themes, which were more present among singer-songwriters (like Joaquín Sabina) and ballad singers.

The encounter between Calamaro and Rot also gives us a glimpse into the origin of the sound of Los Rodríguez. As music sociologist Georgina Born (2005) points out, in a work of art, we can trace the influences of past works and anticipate the traits that will be developed in subsequent works. For example, this encounter originated Calamaro's professed admiration for Gabinete Caligari, as it was Rot who showed him some albums by the Madrilenian band, whose symbolic universe (bullfighting and traditional Spanish popular music) can be detected in Los Rodríguez (Puchades 2003: 125). From a musical point of view, the interaction between Rot and Calamaro established musical patterns that were developed in two of Calamaro's albums on which Rot collaborated, which anticipated the sound of Los Rodríguez: *Por mirarte* (Because I Saw You, 1988) and *Nadie sale vivo de aquí* (Nobody Comes Out of Here Alive, 1989). As mentioned, both musicians were former members of relatively popular bands and then began solo careers marked by typical sounds of the eighties (e.g. synthesizers and programmed drums). Rot joined Calamaro's band as guitarist, producer and composer and, at a musical level, decided to approach rock and roll in a way that moved away from the recording techniques of the eighties, instead favouring a recording process in which all the members of the band played together in the studio.

The first album collaboration between the two musicians was *Por mirarte*, released in 1988. Compared to Calamaro's two previous solo albums (*Hotel Calamaro* and *Vida cruel*, from 1984 and 1985, respectively), this album gave greater prominence to electric guitars and rock and roll music, as can be felt in the Spanish cover of Chuck Berry's classic 'Johnny B. Goode'. Nonetheless, the album's production, drums and certain guitar effects, such as the flanger, are still linked to the aesthetics of the eighties. In terms of musical genre, the album gives us a glimpse of the eclecticism that would become characteristic of Calamaro and Rot throughout their careers: in addition to songs with more of a rock sound, the album contains piano ballads, funk, hard rock and rap. It is also worth noting that the album includes a cover of 'Sin saber qué decir', composed by Ariel Rot and Sergio Makaroff, which Rot had already released on his album *Vértigo*. In comparison to Rot's original song, Calamaro's version is closer to pop-rock and makes more prominent use of electric guitars.

While *Por mirarte* can be understood as an evolution of Calamaro's work, transitioning from New Wave and synthesizers to rock, *Nadie sale vivo de aquí* features some of the elements that eventually characterized the work of Los Rodríguez: riffs and songs linked to the sound of the Rolling Stones, the use of Latin American folk music, the emotional lyrics of Calamaro and the affected voice of the Argentinean. Although the album was not produced solely by Rot, the guitarist participated in the production, played guitar and wrote some of the songs on it. Songs like 'Nadie sale vivo de aquí' (written by Calamaro and Rot), 'Señoritas' and 'Dos Romeos' reflect the influence of classic rock and roll and the Rolling Stones sound on both musicians, as well as their taste for catchy riffs, which would become very present in Los Rodríguez. An interesting decision is the inclusion of the songs 'No tengo tiempo' (I Have No Time) and 'Adiós amigos, adiós' (Goodbye, My Friends, Goodbye), which tentatively introduce rhythms and patterns reminiscent of rancheras and tango and show a taste for hybridization and the reclamation of folklore. On this album, Calamaro's voice is quite prominent, as are the chorus and the backing vocals, traits that also anticipated the style of Los Rodríguez. 'Ni hablar' (Forget It) can also be connected to certain pop songs by Los Rodríguez, such as 'Mi enfermedad' (My Disease), which have clear melodies and catchy choruses. As for the lyrics, Calamaro's songs focus on the emotional fragility caused by break-ups and heartbreak, including 'Nuestro Vietnam' (Our Vietnam), 'Pasemos a otro tema' (Let's Change the Subject), 'Una deuda en el corazón' (Debt of the Heart) and 'Señal que te he perdido' (A Sign That I Have Lost You). Moreover, this album reflects a certain influence of Bruce Springsteen (e.g. in the use of saxophone) and the hard rock of the seventies (e.g. the riff of 'Pero sin sangre' (But without Blood)), which Calamaro further developed later in his career, after Los Rodríguez.

The bassist of Calamaro's band at the time, Alejandro Schanzenbach, recalls that the album was highly praised by critics, but that, given the economic crisis and hyperinflation that was ravaging Argentina at the time, it barely sold any copies. The musician's perspective on the album and Calamaro's band at that time is that 'Los Rodríguez was the continuation of Calamaro's band. They continued with the sound format that we had established. We performed songs like "Tú me estás atrapando otra vez"[2] [You Are Catching Me Again] and it is almost as if it were part of *Nadie sale vivo de aquí*' (quoted in Babas and Turrón 2020: 14).

From Siroco to *Buena suerte* (1990–1)

In Chapter 2, we outlined the social and musical space in which Los Rodríguez emerged, and their position among the dominant music scenes. The group maintained relationships and collaborated with musicians from different scenes (e.g. Rot participated in some of Extremoduro's albums), but its musical approach was more influenced by groups from the eighties, such as Gabinete Caligari, and singer-songwriters, such as Joaquín Sabina. As mentioned, the group managed to gain prestige among contemporary bands thanks to their work ethic, but as had happened with music critics in the seventies, Argentine rock continued to generate a halo of fascination in some spheres of Spanish music in the nineties. For example, some musicians were impressed with Calamaro's solo work, as recalled by Pancho Varona (in Babas and Turrón 2020: 15), the guitarist of Joaquín Sabina's band and composer of many of his songs, who was surprised by the literary quality of the

Argentinean. In the documentary *100 pájaros volando* (100 Birds Flying), Julián Infante states, in a somewhat humorous tone, that 'without Buenos Aires, rock and roll would not have existed in Spain'. Although this assertion may be an exaggeration, we can understand that Infante was trying to claim the legacy of Tequila and Los Rodríguez for rock in Spain. For Germán Vilella:

> What I noticed at that time is that in general, the technical, musical and creative level of Argentine musicians was higher than that of musicians from Spain, and from the rest of the Spanish-speaking world. … Argentina in is a world of its own; its musicians are one step ahead in originality and in technical terms. (Personal communication, 15 June 2019, Figueras)

For his part, David Bonilla had a similar impression, entrenching the idea that Argentine rock was much more established than its Spanish counterpart:

> Argentines have a more elaborate view of rock. The first time I went to Buenos Aires, I realized that rock there was not sporadic, like in Spain. There, it was a movement, 'national nock'. Rock is their music, and it was not like that in Spain. National rock in the nineties was vital and essential for everyone, not only for rock fans. (Personal communication, 29 September 2019, Madrid)

Thanks to their prestige and work ethic, in 1991, after less than a year as a band, Los Rodríguez released its first album, *Buena suerte* (Good Luck), with the record label Pasión. The label was directed by Paco Martín, A&R and artistic director of several record labels. Back in the eighties, Martín had created one of the most important independent labels of that decade, Twins, which signed Hombres G, Rosendo and Los Secretos. At Pasión, Martín also showed his good taste for music, as he signed Antonio Vega, Extremoduro and Los Rodríguez.

The album was recorded following the classic format that Rot and Calamaro had established as a working method in their Argentine phase: the whole group played at the same time, then chorus and tracks were added (Babas and Turrón 2020: 59). A striking fact is that the album was self-produced by the band, also following the pattern of the albums Calamaro made with Rot. Considering that it was their first album, it seems that for the label, the group had an important prestige, so their criteria were respected.

A significant portion of the album was composed by both Calamaro and Rot (five songs). Individually, Calamaro wrote two songs, and Rot and Infante wrote one each. Collectively, the three musicians co-wrote two songs, which reflected the intense work dynamics of the group which would disappear in later albums. Musically, the album condenses the genres and influences that characterized the group throughout its journey. For Germán Vilella,

> Los Rodríguez had a very rock side, a very pop side and a
> hybrid side with general Latin American roots. Each side had
> its own appeal. Three sides with equal importance. (Personal
> communication, 15 June 2019, Figueras)

These three facets of the band can already be detected in its first album: songs linked to rock, with Rolling Stones influences, such as 'La parte de atrás' (The Back Side), 'Canal 69' (Channel 69) and *La mujer de un amigo* (A Friend's Wife), all with powerful riffs and fast tempos. The pop side[3] can be perceived in Calamaro's taste for ballads, like '100 pájaros' (100 Birds) and 'La mirada del adiós' (The Goodbye Look), and pop-rock songs with acoustic guitars, choruses and clear melodies, like 'A los ojos' ('Into Our Eyes') and 'Mi enfermedad' (My Disease). On this album, the hybridization with folk music occurs in 'Engánchate conmigo' (Hook Up with Me), which was created in collaboration with Antonio Flores and combines flamenco and Latin sounds. Chapter 2 addressed the group's link with Lola Flores's son, with whom Germán Vilella had already worked. Flores was the one who introduced the group to the world of *bulerías* (Andalusian songs accompanied by clapping and dancing) and flamenco music, which fascinated Calamaro. In the lyrics, the songs written by Calamaro talk about issues of heartbreak, break-ups and distrust. A good example is the popular line 'mis amigos me dijeron, "Andrés, no te enamores la primera vez"' (my friends told me, 'Andrés, do not fall in love the first time') in 'Engánchate conmigo'.

Following Ogas (2019) on migrant musicians and musical identity, this album by Los Rodríguez reflects a continuity with the approach that Tequila and Moris developed in the seventies. Los Rodríguez are defined, broadly speaking, as a rock and roll band with a raw and direct sound, aligned with what the aforementioned musicians had done. In turn, as Vilella points out, Los Rodríguez were interested in the hybridization of rock with folk music, as well as in more melodic songs and ballads. As Ogas (2019) puts it in characterizing migrant musicians, the sound of Los Rodríguez is 'neither from here, nor from there'. The rock created in the early nineties in Argentina, like in the case of Soda Stereo with 'Canción animal' (Animal Song, 1990), was closer to the alternative rock and grunge that emerged in those years. In the Spanish case, we have already seen that Los Rodríguez did not fit into the main rock scenes. Los Rodríguez searched for their own space to reclaim the musical legacy that their compatriots had built in the seventies. However, the band also exhibited patterns of the two musical cultures they were playing with. They admired groups like Los Fabulosos Cadillacs and songs like Seguridad Social's 'Chiquilla' (Little Girl), and have also recognized the influence of groups such as Gabinete Caligari and genres like New Flamenco. From these diverse influences, their own distinct sound emerged, a different way of looking at Spanish and Argentine culture.

The album had the elements needed to achieve certain public and critical recognition, but it went unnoticed by the general public. Ariel Rot (in Puchades 2003: 140) and Paco Martín (in Babas and Turrón 2020: 69) recall that the album was played on Radio 3, the Spanish public radio station dedicated to popular music, but not on Los 40 Principales, the primary music radio station in the country. Martín points out that Los Rodríguez, being a group of veteran musicians, reminded radio stations of the bands from the seventies and eighties (like Tequila and Gabinete Caligari). David Bonilla explains that this perception of the group was also held by some record label executives:

> With their first album, several colleagues from Warner insisted to the A&R and the director that they should be signed, but at that time, they were seen as an old group. They were thirty-something years old, but it was like a has-been group of veterans. They were perceived as a band that had already had their chance. (Personal communication, 29 September 2019, Madrid)

Even so, the album was praised by important rock critics such as Diego A. Manrique, media outlets such as the newspaper *El*

País and specialized magazines such as *Ruta 66*. The reviews of the album and its live performances made references to the Rolling Stones, the Faces and, of course, Tequila (whose songs Los Rodríguez covered in their early repertoire). In fact, promotional posters highlighted the past of Julián Infante and Ariel Rot in Tequila as a selling point (Babas and Turrón 2020: 87). Therefore, although the album did not achieve success in terms of sales, it gained a certain prestige by attracting the attention of important intermediaries (like critics and A&R) and contemporary groups, who were pleasantly surprised by the band's sound and Andrés Calamaro's sensitive and moving singing style, which suited the tone of the album's lyrics (Babas and Turrón 2020: 72).

Despite its limited public success in Spain, the album gave Los Rodríguez the chance to be heard in Argentina through Fabiana Cantilo, an Argentine rock composer who released a cover of 'Mi enfermedad'. This allowed the band to play in some medium-sized venues in Argentina (Puchades 2003: 140).

Within the scene more connected to rock, some groups did not like Los Rodríguez's integration of folk music. Fernando Martín,[4] then a member of Desperados and later a music critic for *El País*, pointed out: 'The only thing I found questionable about them was their excessive fondness for rumba. I thought that a good rock and roll band like them did not need *verbena* songs to sell records' (in Babas and Turrón 2020: 63). This quote reflects the cultural, ideological and artistic clash between Los Rodríguez and a certain part of the Spanish rock scene. We have already seen how rock in Spain, since the seventies, was developed from the perspective of resistance: rock, with its connections to punk, built a critical yet diffuse discourse on political, economic and social issues, as reflected in such scenes as urban rock, radical Basque rock and punk. In turn, these dynamics of resistance also played out in the critical discourse of the music industry, radio stations and commercially successful groups. It is a classic dynamic in popular music, and in art in general: distrust towards major companies, mass consumption and successful groups.

As Simon Frith (1981) has explained, rock builds a contradictory ideology which embraces mass culture but at the same time defends a 'folk' notion of community and belonging that rejects commercialism. That fine line between authentic and inauthentic has generated numerous discussions and confrontations in popular music. In the case of Los Rodríguez, their discourse and practices placed them in a space different to that of Spanish rock bands. As we saw in the first chapter, rock in Argentina was, since the sixties, a massive cultural form that was not exempt from the debates on authenticity (Alabarces 1992: 44), but its central positioning in the national culture was not in dispute. In Spain, rock has never occupied that space, beyond brief phases in the eighties in which some groups and scenes stood out. In that sense, we can argue that for Spanish rock bands, the musical forms and genres that did occupy central and massive spaces in Spanish culture (ballad singers, folk, pop), based on their presence in the media, in commercial radio stations and in sales figures, were part of a hegemonic culture that should be challenged.

Los Rodríguez's approach departed from these logics in a variety of ways. First, by accepting rock as part of mass culture, just as Rot and Calamaro had experienced it through their enculturation in Argentina, not hiding their economic interests at stake. Something similar happened with Tequila, which got access to a mass audience more quickly than contemporary Spanish groups from the seventies and eighties. It seems that, for Los Rodríguez, getting praise from certain critics was not as important as making a living (the best one possible) from making music. As Lawrence Grossberg (1993) has proposed, ideas about what is authentic and inauthentic in popular music began to be reconsidered in the eighties, leading to the emergence of what this author calls 'authentic inauthenticity': if authenticity is a construct, the only way to show something is true in music is by admitting its falsehood, its 'inauthenticity'. The romantic view of popular music as resistance to capitalism, or as an artistic cultural form with no relation to economic issues, was later replaced by a pragmatic discourse in which those groups that recognized the importance of economic success and fame in their work were accepted as 'authentic'. In the case of Los Rodríguez, we should not view their intentions as restricted to a mere issue of economics. However, when Los Rodríguez are compared to other national bands, we do perceive that their aesthetic approach and their statements about pecuniary issues were clearer, as was their desire to be known and popular, not just for a select audience but among the general public.

From the aesthetic point of view, Martín's criticism of Los Rodríguez's love for *verbenas* reflects a certain elitism on the part of Spanish rock towards popular culture and folk music. *Verbenas* combine folk music, like *chotis* (a traditional dance of Madrid), *pasodoble* and rumba, with bumper cars, food stalls, dance and typical drinks. In some parts of Spain, such as Galicia, *verbenas* feature live music performed by orchestras that cover a wide range of genres, from folk music to current hits and pop and rock classics. As mentioned, not only was Los Rodríguez's music inspired by *verbenas* and closely linked genres (such as rumba), but songs like 'Sin Documentos' also eventually became part of the repertoire of these orchestras. Martín's rejection of this type of music and these spaces also suggests a rejection by part of the Spanish rock scene of hybridization, and of a certain imitation of Anglophone rock. Martín seems to suggest that in order for authentic rock to keep its essence, it should not be hybridized with folk music. This debate, as we will see later, was present within Los Rodríguez: the Spanish musicians (Germán Vilella and Julián Infante) did not feel comfortable doing rumba-rock. In the case of Calamaro and Rot, we have already seen that their albums in Argentina made small incursions into the combination of pop-rock and folk music. In addition, in their previous careers, they had participated in musically hybridized groups (Calamaro in Raíces) or had made brief forays into Latin rock (Rot in some of Tequila's songs). Eventually, the view of the external observer, in the 'game of mirrors' of Spanish culture, outweighed that of the internal observer.

Disco Pirata (1992)

The release of Los Rodríguez's second album, *Disco Pirata*, was somewhat strange. The album is a compilation of live and studio recordings of songs from their first album, along with some covers of songs by Argentine musicians and two new songs: 'No estoy borracho' (I'm Not Drunk) and the instrumental 'Boogie de los piratas' (Pirate Boogie). The concept for this album was not accepted by the Pasión record label, and it ended up being brought out in 1992 by RTVE Música, a subsidiary of the Spanish public radio and television corporation. This record label mainly published orchestral and folk music, not typically rock.

According to the group's manager, Luis Rupérez, this strange move was made with the aim of causing a break with their record label, since the group believed that Pasión did not have enough contacts and the band's work was not reaching a large enough audience (Babas and Turrón 2020: 105). The title of the album seems to play with the idea of rarities and live recordings, the bootlegs which fans record and circulate through fan communities. Calamaro, a great follower of Bob Dylan, could have taken that reference from the countless bootlegs – official and non-official – in circulation of the American musician's work. Indeed, the album plays with the idea of liveness, inserting audience applause and noise between songs. However, not all of the tracks were live recordings, as some were recorded in the studio.

In summary, the album includes four covers of songs from the first album ('Mi enfermedad', 'A los ojos', 'Engánchate conmigo' and 'Canal 69', the latter featuring Argentine musician Fito Páez); a new version of 'Adiós Amigos, Adiós', originally included on Andrés Calamaro's album *Nadie sale vivo de aquí*; three covers of Argentine/Spanish rock; and a new version of 'Copa rota' (Broken Glass), a song by José Alfredo Jiménez also popularized by José Feliciano. For the covers on the album, Los Rodríguez selected two songs already covered by Tequila (Charly García's 'Mr. Jones' and the Makaroff brothers' 'Rock del ascensor'), along with 'Sábado a la Noche', from Moris's Spanish phase. The inclusion of these new versions of songs already known to the Spanish public clearly connected Los Rodríguez with Tequila and Moris, and with their legacy. As we have already mentioned, in the early nineties, both artists seemed to have been forgotten, but Los Rodríguez reclaimed their work. The choice of these covers seemed intended to deepen the connections between Argentine and Spanish rock, but without adding new elements to that connection. In other words, the group used references that were already known and recognized by Spanish fans instead of considering the work of groups and artists who were key in Argentine rock (Spinetta, Sui Generis, Manal) but were not recognized by the Spanish public back then (as is still the case today).

The album did not make too much of an impact among the Spanish public or media, but the group took the opportunity to continue touring in Argentina, where they were increasingly recognized as 'Andrés Calamaro's band' (Babas and Turrón 2020: 120).

The recording of the album *Sin Documentos* (1993)

Even at the demo stage, *Sin Documentos* aimed to become an important album, and the group was aware that the songs they were creating were powerful. However, no record company showed interest in those songs, as they perceived the group to be outdated. After Los Rodríguez made the demos, a year went by before they managed to record the album with the label DRO. During this time, the group became discouraged, and Andrés Calamaro considered the idea of undertaking a solo career in Argentina, where he had received offers from multiple record companies (Babas and Turrón 2020: 133; Puchades 2003: 142).

At the end of 1992, Rupérez sent the demo to Alfonso Pérez, director of DRO Records. Pérez had been part of the pop band Esclarecidos as drummer and lyricist. Along with other bands from the eighties, they had created Grabaciones Accidentales, a record label that signed successful groups at that time, such as Duncan Dhu, Los Burros and Los Enemigos. As Pérez explains:

DRO resulted from the merger of three labels. One was Grabaciones Accidentales, where I come from. The second one was DRO, which is the label driven by the band Aviador Dro. At one point, Grabaciones Accidentales bought shares from DRO, because we were the small ones, but we started selling a lot of Duncan Dhu records. There was a split between the owners of DRO, and we took advantage of it and entered as shareholders. Afterwards, Grabaciones Accidentales and DRO bought Twins, the third label, which had Hombres G. And then it was time for the merger of DRO and Grabaciones Accidentales. (Personal communication, 15 October 2019, Madrid)

In 1992, Warner acquired DRO but maintained its autonomy. In Pérez's words:

DRO was owned by Warner but was operated by its original team. DRO had separate headquarters from Warner; it had the same president, but he let us work. In fact, I know Warner said no to Los Rodríguez, but I signed them.

Therefore, the demo of *Sin Documentos* had already gone to Warner, and they were not interested. In contrast, Alfonso Pérez's decision to sign the group was instantaneous:

On 24 December, their manager brought me a demo.
I picked it up, went to do my last-minute shopping and
put it on. And by the third song, I said we would sign them.
There were six songs, including 'Sin documentos' [Without
Documents], 'Salud, dinero y amor' [Health, Money and Love],
'Dulce condena' [Sweet Sentence]. I immediately decided to
sign them, and when I got back from the Christmas holiday,
I spoke to the manager.

The group's arrival at DRO/Warner caused a clash between the two labels, just as they had merged. Alfonso Pérez's bet on the group, and the success it had, served to strengthen DRO's position within Warner:

> I had a problem because the president of Warner did not want to sign them. So, I told him I would leave the company. It was a give-and-take relationship. He had arguments and said, 'We bought you, you have a lot of artists. Why do you need another one?' I had to be strong because I thought, 'If I accept this, I accept everything'. I played it hard, and Los Rodríguez succeeded, although I did not really know them. I knew they had released a record, but I had not paid attention to it. However, I argued that those songs were going to be historic, one way or another.

The album was recorded between April and May 1993 at Eurosonic, one of the most prestigious studios of the time, where Joaquín Sabina, Los Enemigos, Luz Casal and Barricada recorded. The album was once again produced by the group in collaboration with Nigel Walker, the British engineer and producer who had collaborated with George Martín and important English-singing pop-rock groups. The link between Walker, who later settled in Spain, and Los Rodríguez originated from his collaboration with Fito Páez's celebrated album *El amor después del amor* (Love after Loving), on which Andrés Calamaro also collaborated. According to both the group and the producer (in Babas and Turrón 2020: 129), the band prepared the songs very well, while the producer focused more on the technical issues. Both the producer and the band had the Rolling Stones' album *Start Me Up*, with an almost lo-fi sound, in mind as their model.

It is important to address the choice of Walker as producer of an album that aimed to hybridize rock and rumba. As a producer, Walker was not known for albums that sought fusion, but it was somewhat common for British and North American producers to work on Spanish albums that aimed for this kind of hybridization. For example, Joe Dworniak produced important albums for Radio Futura, Jarabe de Palo and Kiko Veneno, while the North American Joey Blaney produced the subsequent albums of Los Rodríguez and Andrés Calamaro. Why not work with local producers? In the case of Spanish rock, many important groups, like Tequila, Barón Rojo, Leño and Héroes del Silencio, had recorded successful albums with foreign producers and studios, looking for a better sound. In the case of albums that sought hybridization with Spanish or Latin folk music, the presence of English and American producers can be interpreted as a search for the Anglophone legitimation of these hybridizations. – a form of validation from those who were formed in the United States and England, the centres of rock culture.

Compared to the previous albums, *Sin Documentos* achieved considerable sales, although less than their later records. According to Alfonso Pérez, the album has sold about 170,000 copies in Spain and 50,000 in Argentina, although in a context in which record sales were quite elevated.

One of the keys to the album's success is its title track 'Sin Documentos', a sort of rumba-rock with passionate lyrics, which fit in with the model of Spanish rumbas by groups such as Los Chichos and Los Chunguitos. The song's origin story has been told by Andrés Calamaro in several interviews (Babas and Turrón 2020: 131; Larocca 2018), from which we can draw some conclusions. In his previous albums (from his solo career and with Los Rodríguez), Calamaro had already shown his interest in the fusion of rock and pop with folk music. Moreover, as a listener, since his arrival in Spain (and even before, through Ariel Rot), Calamaro had been interested in groups such as Gabinete Caligari, Los Chichos and the bands of the 'Caño Roto sound'.[5] Calamaro had also developed a relationship, through Los Rodríguez, with New Flamenco artists such as Ray Heredia and La Barbería del Sur. Likewise, Argentine groups such as Los Fabulosos Cadillacs are also cited as inspiration.

It is interesting that another influence Calamaro identifies is a hit song of that time, 'Chiquilla', by the Valencian group Seguridad Social. The band, which was linked to punk sounds, had evolved since the late eighties towards the hybridization of Latin sounds with rock. 'Chiquilla' was a hit song in 1991 and, like 'Sin Documentos', is a popular song for outdoor festivals and compilations of the best of Spanish pop songs.[6] Both songs begin with recognizable riffs, which evoke indigenous sounds, and use the Andalusian or Phrygian cadence in their chords. This progression is a 'cadence structure typical not just of Andalusian music but of all Spanish music. … It appears in the popular repertoire of all Spain and has been used as an idiomatic element by national and foreign composers alike' (Casares 1999: 860). The cadence is formed by the chord progression of A minor, G major, F major and E major. As musicologist Celsa Alonso (2010: 209) has explained, this cadence has been used on multiple occasions in Spanish pop-rock when constructing a sound discourse related to Spanish culture. In the case of Seguridad Social and Los Rodríguez, both songs take some liberties in applying the scale.[7] In 'Chiquilla', the chords are in a higher key, in F major, and seem to be performed as power chords, which is characteristic of punk rock. 'Sin Documentos' also starts from a higher key, G minor, and the guitars play the syncopated sounds of the *ventilador*[8] technique, typical of rumba.

For Germán Vilella, the main difference between the two songs is the rhythmic aspect:

> The rhythm of 'Chiquilla' was rock. What was rumba about it was its harmony, the singing style and the Andalusian scale, but the rhythm was rock. Los Rodríguez were the first group that made a change to the rhythm, to the base of rumba, with the snare drum that I introduced, which was half rockabilly, half rumba. The bass drum was rumba, like in all the songs by Los Chichos. And the guitar technique that Julián was doing was the *ventilador*, totally. Individually, none of the instruments was very innovative, so for me, the success it achieved was quite puzzling. (Personal communication, 15 June 2019, Figueras)

Although Calamaro has explained the song as something he came up with, we can see that both the drummer and the guitarist played key roles in the creative process. Calamaro was not the only member interested in hybridization, or the only one with knowledge of such music. Ariel Rot points out that in his shared phase with Calamaro in Argentina, they shared an interest in Los Fabulosos Cadillacs and tango, and he got to know the work of Los Chunguitos on his own and even composed a song for the flamenco singer Tijeritas (Puchades 2003: 127). As for Vilella, we have already noted that the drummer had played with rumba groups and had a relationship with musicians from these scenes:

> I was very close to Ketama and Navajita Plateá … the first years of Los Rodríguez, and before that, I moved around bars, like El Cardamomo, where people like Ray Heredia performed. Improvisations were done there, and I played the cajón [box

drum]. And they said to me: 'How can this *payo*[9] play like that?'
I never liked that we introduced rumba in Los Rodríguez.
I did not like it enough to play it myself. What I really like is a
saeta, a *seguidilla*, a *bulería* and *cante jondo*.[10] My grandfather
is from Jaén, so I love flamenco. I burst into tears when I listen
to Camarón de la Isla. … To me, *rumba* and *sevillana* songs
are frivolous and superficial. I feel like the best of the Spanish
musical heritage was dismissed.

It is striking that for Vilella, playing certain folk music genres
in a rock group was not interesting. From Vilella's perspective
on Spanish folk music, which was deeper than Calamaro's, the
fusion of rock and rumba was frivolous:

In the first album we already did 'Engánchate conmigo',
where the rhythm is the same as in 'Sin documentos'. I did
the rhythm of the drummers in Los Chunguitos then. I did
not like it very much. But when they came to me with 'Sin
documentos', I said, 'Not another one! What should I do? …
I do not want to do the Chunguitos thing again…'. So, what
I was doing on the hi-hat, I did it on the snare drum. Andrés
Calamaro was interested in all that stuff. He was the one who
brought it to the group. Julián also liked it. Well, more than
that, he was amused by the rumba scene, and he was very
good at it. But Julián liked rock, like me. We were not in favour
of playing rumba in the band.[11] Julián and I are the ones who
know how to play rumba, but we were the ones who did not
like it. For the other two, it seemed like a very curious style. It's
as if I arrived in Argentina and said, 'I'm going to play a tango'.
Those in the group would say to me, 'Stop fucking around'.
Argentines have a lot of respect for tango. That is why I have
great respect for flamenco music.

As for Moris with the everyday life of Spanish society, Calamaro's perspective as a foreigner, with his somewhat unprejudiced view of flamenco and rumba, allowed him to make innovations that, as Vilella proposes, could seem frivolous to Spaniards. Despite Vilella's reservations, his work, just like Infante's, was fundamental in the development of the song, as he knew the structures and techniques of rumba. Over the years, Vilella has come to value the song to a greater extent:

> Now I like the song, but the riff at the beginning reminded me of what I have heard all my life at fairs, with Ferris wheels and bumper cars. I could not stand it. Then the melody, the lyrics, the way Andrés sang it, the charisma … all that made sense. But the riff, when I heard it the first time, I said, 'This can't be real'.

For Alfonso Pérez, the song had an important impact and ended up overshadowing an album with many other great songs:

> It's not because 'Sin documentos' was a rumba, but for me, it isn't the best song on the record. There are many songs that are a blast. But yeah, the song eclipsed the record a bit. (Personal communication, 15 October 2019, Madrid)

David Bonilla agrees on this issue:

> When an artist puts out an album and has a major success with a single, the rest of the songs are left on a secondary plane. It happened to 'Sin documentos'. 'Dulce condena' (Sweet Sentence) is an amazing track, but people only remember 'Sin documentos'. An enormous success eclipses

the rest of the songs. This particularly happens in the eyes of the mainstream audience, a superficial public that only knows what is playing on the radio and not much else. (Personal communication, 29 September 2019, Madrid)

A key point in understanding the relative success of the album is that it was picked up by radio stations, such as Los 40 Principales. Indeed, one of the reasons why the group left their first Spanish record label was because of the sense that it did not have access to important media, an issue that Alfonso Pérez fully resolved at DRO:

> They had not been played on the radio. And that time, I went to introduce the single to Los 40 Principales, which I did not usually do. I told them, 'Listen to this song, and if you do not think it will be a number one, do not play it', so they played it, and it became number one for I don't know how many weeks. It was played a lot. (Personal communication, 15 October 2019, Madrid)

David Bonilla explains the importance of being played on Los 40 Principales:

> To be played on Los 40 Principales was a guarantee of success. When a group would put out a record and the doorman would say, 'I heard you on the radio', he meant Los 40 Principales. Everyone knew the new songs through this station. Radio had important power to achieve success, it gave songs popularity, but then, there are many other things to do. The song must have the capacity to engage people. It may be played a lot and yet not engage. (Personal communication, 29 September 2019, Madrid)

A song-by-song review of *Sin Documentos*

Their rock attitude, melodic ability and intense performance on stage made Los Rodríguez an essential group for understanding the Spanish musical scene during their brief existence, and especially afterwards. Germán Vilella said at the time that *Sin Documentos* was a rock treatise, due to the band's variety of styles and ability to handle hybridization without sounding like an exercise in style. Attentive listening to the songs on the album corroborates this statement.

The song that opens the album, '**Pequeño salto mortal**' (Little Leap of Faith, a title that refers to 'Jumpin' Jack Flash' by Jagger and Richards), lays claim to the heritage of Tequila. Rock and roll had not been a genre used during *La Movida Madrileña*, but as we have seen, their admiration for the Rolling Stones and classic guitar groups of the sixties connected Los Rodríguez with the groups that made the bridge between *La Movida Madrileña* and the Malasaña sound, such as Los Ronaldos. Composed by Rot and Calamaro, 'Pequeño salto mortal' is a Rolling Stones–style rock and roll track, with percussive barrelhouse piano and guitar licks inherited from Keith Richards's style. In the second half, the song is driven by a powerful wind section that adds a touch of soul.

The lyrics exemplify Calamaro's way of seeing love: challenge, co-dependency, suffering. It is full of images that depict a powerful woman whose man is a prisoner who must be fed and satiated: only the closeness of the woman he loves makes him feel powerful and feel 'the wind in his sails'. In the introduction to the book that journalist Darío Manrique dedicated to Calamaro's 1999 album *Honestidad brutal* (Brutal Honesty), Argentine psychoanalyst Jorge Alemán explains that

Calamaro did something no other Argentine musician had achieved: 'to touch the Spanish adolescent soul' through a lyrical character, 'an abandoned man who lets his melancholic inspiration speak without limits' (in Manrique 2014: X). This character has a strong presence throughout the album and, as we have seen, is rooted in the Argentine rock tradition and influenced by tango masculinity.

'**Hasta que el sueño venga**' (Until I Fall Asleep) shows the wide musical background and varied styles of Los Rodríguez in less than four minutes. After a brief dialogue between the organ and the electric guitar, the verse starts with syncopated rhythms, in the style of a slow reggae, while the chorus has the air of a pop ballad. Once again, a brutal vision of love guides the lyrics: the beloved becomes an obsession, a memory that is evoked 'once and a thousand times' in that imprecise moment that separates sleep from wakefulness. That memory, which makes him climb up the walls, never disappears. Despite the pain, the singer would give almost everything to repeat that moment.

The song evolves in the second part: after repeating the title phrase several times with increasing intensity and the support of the backing vocals, which seems to announce the end, a long, psychedelic guitar solo starts, while Calamaro makes guttural sounds as if improvising in a jam session. Then the piano repeats a phrase with an unmistakable salsa sound a couple of times, and then the singer sings the first lines of the classic flamenco song 'Soy gitano' (I Am a Gypsy), by Camarón de la Isla. In less than two minutes, the listener has gone from the Rolling Stones to flamenco, passing through Cuban music and psychedelia.

In **'Dulce condena'** (Sweet Sentence), Rot and Calamaro demonstrate their ability to create energetic pop songs. In the face of Calamaro's mournful attitude, this song is a celebration of love: it is a sweet sentence suffered by those who like problems and dare to 'start from scratch', to make room for 'a new illusion' and to give love another chance. The tripartite structure of the song, with a verse, a bridge and a chorus, is repeated three times with slight variations: the chorus, with a clear melody, is framed in a game of obbligatos from the guitars and organ that add strength and rock personality, supported in the final part by the sudden appearance of an extended guitar solo that, once again, claims the legacy of the Rolling Stones. This combination of catchy melodies and a rock attitude is what made people in the Spain of the nineties sing Los Rodríguez songs in all the bars and *verbenas*.

'Sin Documentos' (Without Documents), in addition to being the album's title track, was the song that rocketed Los Rodríguez to popularity. It is another showcase of the breadth of musical knowledge and diverse musical experiences of all the band's members, as well as their openness to external influences. As we have already seen, the rhythm is basically a rumba, a style derived from flamenco that became popular in the working-class neighbourhoods of Madrid and Barcelona at a time when rural immigration was accelerating the development of those cities. The song starts right away with the drums which, as we have already highlighted, had been very influential in the evolution of Latin rock: 'Vilella created that style … transitioning the guitar strokes [typical of rumba] to the snare drum' (Lichis, in Babas and Turrón 2020: 185).

Moreover, the unmistakable guitar riff creates a bridge between rock and rumba. Once the voice enters, there is an interesting dialogue between the electric guitars with the percussive *ventilador* rhythm, typical of rumba, and the piano with a Latin feel. Let's not forget that Calamaro played piano in the candombe-rock band Raíces as a young musician, while Rot has emphasized Julián Infante's great rhythmic abilities: 'with his left hand, he was not one to do great solos or anything virtuosic, but with the right hand, he did things that very few can do. He played rumbas like no one else, with a very loose right hand' (in Babas and Turrón 2020: 21).

The structure of the song is typical of pop-rock, with verse, bridge and chorus. In the bridges, the guitar departs from the rumba style and performs a brief riff in the background, which is reminiscent of the pioneering rock approaches to flamenco by Los Brincos in the sixties with songs like 'Flamenco' and 'A mi con esas' (Don't Give Me That Bullshit). The flamenco-like quality of the song is reinforced with clapping in the background. It also makes use of *jaleos* to increase the song's intensity, something else that had already been done by Los Brincos. *Jaleos* are brief spoken expressions to cheer on the artist or the audience, like the *¡Ahí vamos!* (Here we come!) that gives way to the introductory riff of 'Sin Documentos'.

The chorus uses the classic call-and-response structure of rumba: the (male) chorus repeats the first and third lines, while Calamaro sings the other two lines solo. Once this pattern has been repeated twice, the song gains its rock demeanour with an unusually long string-bending guitar solo. Two traits of Los Rodríguez's music are present in their biggest hit: the ability to fuse different styles and influences within a rock framework, and the intensity that makes all the songs build more and more from beginning to end.

In the emotional anguish so typical of flamenco (which rumba does not reject), Calamaro finds a mirror through which to develop his vision of romantic relationships. It is an inspiration at once desperate and heroic, a *carpe diem* driven by the tragic conviction that the end is near: the line 'I have no other intentions than to continue drinking from this glass that is not so broken' is a reference to the tango song 'Copa rota' (Broken Glass) featured on *Disco pirata*. 'Sin Documentos' speaks of a very strong pain that never ends ('I die while I wait for you') and the inability to give in to pleasure given the certainty of the pain that will come.

The next song on the album changes the subject: Ariel Rot's hedonistic **'Na, na, na'**, which once again reflects the band's inheritance from Tequila. It is a rock and roll track with guitar riffs and boogie piano, with lyrics that make puns on things related to concerts and tours (payments, maps, contracts). The hedonistic celebration ('bring the alcohol, bring sunglasses') is spoilt by a woman's betrayal (the girl with a dagger, 'You took my money, and you took the stuff'). It is, in a way, the road movie of *Sin Documentos*: rock concerts, dangerous women, parties and drugs – the mention of *tiros* (shots) might refer to gunshots, but it was also a slang term for cocaine in Madrid's nightlife. It is a song that invites the audience to participate with its 'Na na na', which the whole band chants non-stop in the last part of the song.

In an instant, the album goes from summer abandon to the domestic intimacy of **'7 Segundos'** (7 Seconds), which opens with the slowed-down notes of 'Jingle Bells' to create a nostalgic atmosphere centring on the piano, supported by string arrangements in the bridge sections. The drums appear only for a few moments at the end, preceded by another brief section in which the voice dialogues with the bass to give way, again, to 'Jingle Bells'.

Calamaro shows his skill as a lyricist by incorporating many local references: Canal Plus, the first pay television channel in Spain, which launched in those same years; El Corte Inglés, the workplace of the female protagonist and the largest department store chain in Spain; and the Austral Plan, an initiative of the Argentine government to solve inflation that pushed many Argentines, like the protagonist of the song, to emigrate. As Moris had done in the seventies, Calamaro makes an important contribution to the hybrid identity of Los Rodríguez by mixing references to the reality and popular culture of both Spain and Argentina. In this song, we can see how Calamaro's identity is being forged between two spaces: 'I always say that I'm bilingual; I write the songs in a slang that is not understood in Madrid or in Buenos Aires, the slang of transoceanic round-trip flights' (Calamaro, in Manrique 2014: 61). Again, this supports Julio Ogas's (2019) idea that the cultural identity that musicians build is not from any single place and, thus, may be understood neither in Argentina nor in Spain.

It is tempting to read the lyrics as inspired by the biography of Calamaro himself, an Argentine who migrated to Spain and was trapped in a love affair that, once again, was doomed to failure and sadness. '7 Segundos' is a strange and sad Christmas carol that shares the depressing atmosphere of the Pogues's classic 'Fairytale of New York' (Warner 1988), released a few years earlier. The song is also reminiscent of the grey, costumbrist atmosphere of the lyrics of 'Rebajas de enero' (January Sales) (BMG/Ariola 1985) by Joaquín Sabina, who was a lyrical influence for the band, as mentioned earlier.

All that sadness is left behind in the feel-good track '**Salud, dinero y amor**' (Health, Money and Love), an authentic tavern song, a toast among friends and a celebration of life and *fiesta*. The music is dominated by the accordion, which sets the entire song in a rhythm reminiscent of the Colombian *joropo* and *son jarocho* (a style of folk music from Veracruz, Mexico), with Germán Vilella evoking from the drum set the characteristic *zapateados* of hardwood floor dance. Here, for once, Calamaro leaves behind his mournful vein and indulges in pleasure and boundless celebration ('I toast for winning, drawing and losing'). The evocation of a tavern is emphasized by the collective chorus that ends each of the verses in a call-and-response mode.

While the previous two songs were driven by a clear feeling, **'Mi rock perdido'** (My Missing Rock) is more ambivalent and complex. Musically, it has a very clear melodic structure driven by guitars that, again, refer to the tradition of the sixties and converse with a retro organ sound that is kept in the background. There is a radical change in the last third of the song, however: two verses in which Calamaro sings in falsetto, the guitars use the characteristic resonance of the flanger effect and soft choruses add a tone reminiscent of the Beatles' *Rubber Soul* (EMI 1965).

This fragment accentuates the tone of emotional fragility present throughout the song: Calamaro is shown afraid to compose, in search of a song that does not arrive, an inspiration that forces him to question his vital signs (the vices and sacrifices of the first two lines), a musical culture – rock – that does not seem to offer him enough material to give shape to his ideas (the rock of lions and lambs, off-limits and non-existent women). This is a surprising statement coming from an artist who, a few years later, would deliver a 37-song album (*Honestidad brutal*, Dro East West, 1999) followed by an even longer one with 103 songs (*El salmón*, Dro East West, 2000).

In the psychedelic fragment of the song, the author acknowledges that he does not like songs because they are made of turmoil and sensations. From beneath the feel-good, melodic musical garb, the mournful author emerges again. He comes to realize that he makes music to escape from a reality that disturbs him, although it never turns out to be a sufficient remedy.

However, Calamaro is not the only one whose songs portray the tension between happiness and pain. In **'Tú me estás atrapando otra vez'** (You Are Catching Me Again), Julián Infante and Ariel Rot composed a ballad with a blues structure, driven by arpeggiated guitar chords. The lyrics play with continuous contrasts between what should be and what is: 'I should leave you … but you're catching me again'. Love and hate, desire and reality, what is good versus what is desirable. While the lyrics do not clearly identify the object of desire, it is hard to avoid thinking that the addiction is not to a woman, but to drugs. Both Rot and Infante were hooked on heroin, and Infante's early death was due to complications from AIDS. The line 'I get in your car and let life pass me by' may well portray a trip to the ghettos on the periphery of Madrid to get drugs, although the mastery of the composition lies precisely in its ambivalence: it could be a junkie's allegation or the description of a toxic love relationship.

'Mala suerte' (Bad Luck) shows us a Calamaro very much influenced by Dylan. It is a song about a gambler, once again subjected to the existential agony of having to choose, but this time between good luck in gambling or in love. However, this gambler comes to serve as a metaphor for any kind of existence on the edge. Like the previous song, it is a paean to addiction: the man gambles constantly and loses, but he always thinks that he could have won. He bends but never breaks.

Musically, it is a rock song dominated by Rot's guitars, without a clear chorus. The most interesting fragment is located between the two verses and has two distinct parts. The two opening lines rest on soft doo-wop backing vocals that interact with the piano. Roy Orbison's 'Dream Baby' (Monument, 1962) could be a reference here. The following lines are supported by a ternary rhythm that evokes Latin folklore. Calamaro's accent and the brief sound reference interact with the working-class tone of the story to suddenly place it in the tango scene of Buenos Aires.

'Algo se está rompiendo' (Something Is Breaking) is the most rhythmic song of the entire album. The lyrics are more recited than sung, the drums and bass govern the song and the winds and backing vocals play a remarkable role. It is a funk song with a depressing message: love does not last, and this renders everything else meaningless.

In contrast, the album closes with **'Especies que desaparecen'** (Species That Disappear), a peaceful song that starts with a melodic piano alongside guitar arpeggios and the drummer hitting the rim of the snare drum to create a jazzy atmosphere. The chorus, however, is pure Los Rodríguez rock: a powerful melody, evocative lyrics and energetic rhythm, with the organ supporting the voice and the guitars playing in the purest Rolling Stones style. The last part of the song breaks from the verse-chorus structure and the rock sound by introducing a binary rhythm that the voice also executes, which gives it a tropical atmosphere.

The whole second half of the song alternates between the marked binary rhythm and instrumental interludes, first with a blues-jazz guitar solo and then with the piano in the same tone, which gives the leading role back to the guitar. After repeating 'may that never happen between us', Los Rodríguez once again play with the dynamics of the song, lowering the volume and energy of the band to allow the piano and the guitar arpeggios to shine. The organ that maintains the melodic tension gives way to the bandoneon for a few bars in the final part, as if

Calamaro wanted to emphasize his Argentineness with this slight wink at the end of the album.

The song that closes the album highlights the aching tone of Calamaro's apocalyptic view of love: those who love each other are a species doomed to extinction, because it is normal for love to disappear. Hence the singer's desperate tone towards his beloved: 'please, don't leave me', because after our love, there is nothing left but emptiness and loneliness.

The reception of *Sin Documentos*

This album gave Los Rodríguez the opportunity to do more concerts, especially in the summer of 1993. Coincidentally or not, their agency, Rumor, managed three artists that took rumba as a starting point in many of their compositions, although from different perspectives: Rosario Flores, Manolo Tena and Los Rodríguez. That summer tour culminated with Manolo Tena's concert at Las Ventas, with Los Rodríguez as the opening act. Its 2020 release as a live album included material that had already been released on previous compilations.

Many of the group's concerts were commissioned by local governments. In fact, until the crisis of 2008, a fundamental pillar of the Spanish music industry had been the hiring of popular bands by local administrations for patron saint festivities, especially in the summer. These practices led to significant imbalances in the music scenes, since for many groups it was more profitable to play at *verbenas*, working for the municipalities, than to play at venues in those same locations. This practice had a negative impact on venues, and on the consolidation of circuits and scenes, beyond the summer tours. In that sense, according to their manager (quoted in

Babas and Turrón 2020: 158), Los Rodríguez did not have a huge following. In Madrid, they played in medium-capacity venues (of about two thousand people), and outside Madrid their following was smaller, so being hired by municipalities was a very positive thing for them.

In Argentina, the group had a certain success, as it managed to perform five nights in a row at the Gran Rex Theatre (Puchades 2003: 148).[12] However, Germán Vilella thinks the impact of the group in Argentina was exaggerated:

> Andrés Calamaro had made a name for himself there. A concert for a hundred people there made the same noise as a thousand here, and that might make you think you have conquered Argentina. We came back from there feeling like we had been very successful. And our manager, when we came back, said we had sold out. But we played for a hundred, two hundred people. In sales, however, it was the same there as here. And in both sites, *Sin documentos* sold well. (Personal communication, 15 June 2019, Figueras)

As for the critical reception of the album, the reviews were positive. As Babas and Turrón (2020: 152) have documented, the album was positively scored by *Rockdelux*, *Ruta 66* and *El País*. As David Bonilla recalls:

> Los Rodríguez always had very good press. I remember good articles on *Ruta 66*, *Primera Línea*, *Popular 1*, even on *Rockdelux*. It was a group loved by the press. And in *El País*, and its music supplement *El País de las Tentaciones*, which was very important for the music scene, Los Rodríguez were always very well represented and well treated. (Personal communication, 29 September 2019, Madrid)

In retrospective terms, *Sin Documentos* has been featured on most of the critics' compilations of the best Spanish pop-rock albums. Even though the group's previous and subsequent albums included important songs and had higher sales, music critics considered *Sin Documentos* their primary contribution to Spanish popular music. *Rolling Stone* was among the magazines that placed the greatest emphasis on making these lists. The Spanish edition of the magazine (1999–2015) published several lists on which Los Rodríguez were featured prominently. In 2012, the magazine placed Los Rodríguez in a prominent seventh place on its list of the fifty best Spanish rock bands and pointed out that 'they played good Latin rock and roll with a high dose of Spanish identity'. *Rolling Stone*'s list of the 200 best Spanish pop-rock songs also included 'Sin Documentos' at number 22 and 'Dulce condena' at 59. Moreover, the magazine also included *Sin Documentos* at number 25 on its list of the fifty best Spanish rock albums, highlighting its importance in the rebirth of the group and the relevance of its title track as a work of rumba-rock, along with a handful of other exceptional songs.

EfeEme magazine included *Sin Documentos* at number 29 on its list of the 100 best Spanish pop albums, pointing to 'the mixture of blues, rock'n'roll, joropo and Buenos Aires ballads'. For this magazine, Los Rodríguez were 'the Latin American equivalent of the Rolling Stones in *Exile on Main St.* and *Sticky Fingers*'. In its special twenty-fifth anniversary issue (2010), *Ruta 66* included Los Rodríguez's 1991 debut album as one of the most important albums of that year. Likewise, the twentieth anniversary issue of *Rockdelux* placed *Sin Documentos* at number 61 in the 100 best Spanish albums of the twentieth century. In the description of the album, journalist Joan Pons defined Los Rodríguez as heirs of the cross between rock and Latin American sounds initiated by Los Coyotes and Radio Futura. For this journalist, this legacy is 'easy to spoil, as in the case of Seguridad Social, and hard to turn into a 100% Hispanic-American translation of a 100% Anglo-Saxon music, as in the case of Los Rodríguez'. As we can see, Spanish music critics highlighted the importance of Los Rodríguez's approach to musical fusion, and the comparison made in *Rockdelux* is particularly interesting in this regard. For Pons, there are hybridizing formulas that legitimize such an approach, as achieved by Los Rodríguez, Los Coyotes and Radio Futura, and those that delegitimize it, such as Seguridad Social. As we have seen, the approach of Seguridad Social was connected to punk rock, which perhaps has a lower artistic value for critics than that of Los Rodríguez.

On its website, the music outlet *La Fonoteca*[13] makes the case that each one of the songs on *Sin Documentos* 'could be a potential single: the repertoire is masterful'. *La Fonoteca* proposes that the dominance of rock and roll, as well as joropo and candombe in '*Salud, dinero y amor*', makes you think 'that the group could set a stadium on fire and win over a pub's crowd by playing rancheras or tangos acoustically'. Therefore, for the critics, even though the album was marked by its title track, it was a solid compendium in which rock had an important presence, in addition to fusion. In turn, we see that for critics, another positive aspect of the group was its ability to bring together diverse audiences – the majority, which would go to a stadium, and the minority, which would meet in a smaller venue.

Several books on Spanish pop-rock have also highlighted the importance of this album (Lesende and Neira 2006; Ordovás 2010). In his review of the album, journalist Lino Portela praised the value of its musical hybridization, which goes beyond rock: 'In addition to the Rolling Stones heritage

… Los Rodríguez threw on the stew seasonings that were more typical of rumba and candombe … they took rock and wrapped it with a Latin American essence' (in Lesende and Neira 2006: 300). Coinciding with *La Fonoteca*'s criticism, this book also highlighted that the album was played 'in beach bars, trendy disco-pubs and town squares'. Hybridization and access to diverse audiences and spaces were identified as central elements of the album. Finally, it is important to note that the song has been featured on television programmes, such as *La mejor canción jamás cantada* (The Best Song Ever Sung), broadcast by the Spanish Television Network (TVE).[14]

From massive success to the dissolution of Los Rodríguez

Nonetheless, all this praise came at a time when the brotherhood of the group had lost its initial strength. Calamaro's status had grown, and his compulsive nature as a composer had begun to show. He was the sole author of eight of the songs on the album, while on the first album the songs had been co-written by Rot and Calamaro to a greater extent. The same year *Sin Documentos* was released, DRO published the first volume of *Grabaciones encontradas* (Mixed Recordings), which featured previously unreleased material recorded by Calamaro and some covers. Volume 2 of this compilation was released just a year later. Calamaro's production was already remarkable in his solo career in Argentina (four albums in five years), and with Los Rodríguez the pace of production was also fast. However, after the dissolution of the group, Calamaro began a solo career that culminated in two key works: *Honestidad brutal* (1999) and *El salmón* (2000), with 37 and 103 songs, respectively.

Calamaro's compositional voracity and his apparent interest in resuming his solo career affected the hierarchies within the group, which resulted in disagreements surrounding the distribution of royalties for record sales and the money received for live performances, which in turn led to a rift between the members (Babas and Turrón 2020: 200; Puchades 2003: 149). According to Germán Vilella, for their next album, *Palabras más, palabras menos* (1995), the distribution of royalties was 40 per cent for Calamaro, 30 per cent for Rot, 20 per cent for Vilella and 10 per cent for Infante. These percentages were adjusted for live shows so that Infante could receive about 15 per cent.

Palabras más, palabras menos once again contained a majority of songs written by Calamaro, although an agreement was reached so that Rot and Calamaro alternated in the singles that were released (Babas and Turrón 2020: 205). The album's biggest attraction is the songs composed by Rot, especially 'La milonga del marinero y el capitán' (The Milonga of the Sailor and the Captain) and 'Mucho mejor' (Much Better). The former takes up the fusion of rock with milonga, a genre linked to Argentina and Uruguay. The release of the latter as a single was delayed until 1996 to try to turn it into a summer hit (Puchades 2003: 155). Calamaro's song 'Para no olvidar' (Unforgettable), with the collaboration of flamenco guitarist Raimundo Amador, is another example of the group's approach to Spanish popular music.

This album had a higher recording budget than their previous works. It was recorded in El Cortijo, a luxurious studio located in Malaga, and mixed in Madrid and Miami. The production was led by American producer Joe Blaney, who had already worked with Charly García and would later work with Calamaro on his solo albums. This recording broke with the work dynamic that Rot and Calamaro had constructed since their time in Argentina: given the existing tensions, each member recorded their parts separately instead of all at once.

The sales of this album were higher than *Sin Documentos*, selling 200,000 records in Spain, 150,000 in Argentina and 25,000 in the rest of the world (Babas and Turrón 2020: 229).

Joaquín Sabina intersected with the career of Los Rodríguez once again in 1996 when he invited them to tour with him, which turned out to be the group's farewell. Both Andrés Calamaro and Ariel Rot had co-written songs with Sabina, like 'Todavía una canción de amor' (Still a Love Song), with lyrics by Sabina and music by Calamaro, which was included on *Palabras más, palabras menos*. Rot also wrote the music for two of Sabina's songs, 'Jugar por jugar' (Play for Play) and 'Viridiana', released on the album *Yo, mi, me, contigo* (I, My, Me, with You). Throughout the tour, during Sabina's set, Rot and Calamaro came out to sing 'Con la frente marchita' ('With a Withered Forehead') and 'Princesa' (Princess) with him (Babas and Turrón 2020: 274). Symbolically, we can see how one of the first songs that Los Rodríguez played in their first rehearsal, 'Princesa', served as an epilogue for the band and became the song that, twenty-three years later, the band would choose to re-record (without Julián Infante) in a tribute album to Sabina.

In popular music, a common trope when talking about band separations is to state that the band separated at its best. This is accurate in the case of Los Rodríguez, at least in terms of sales, since their best-selling album is the compilation *Hasta luego* (See You Later), which was released in 1996 and sold more than 800,000 copies. The album served as a farewell, featuring new live versions of some songs ('Mi enfermedad', 'Mucho mejor', 'Extraño') and some demos. According to Alfonso Pérez,

The real success was the compilation. It happened by chance. Saul Tagarro, head of Warner, said that the group had much more fame and singles than records sold, and asked why they had not made a greatest hits album. They liked the idea; we made a track listing and released it in a month. (Personal communication, 15 October 2019, Madrid)

The legacy of Los Rodríguez

As we have seen, Los Rodríguez are a valued band in Spanish and Argentine popular music. Music critics have highlighted the importance of their albums, and their songs are still played on the radio and at local festivals. The publication of an oral history of the group, by Kike Babas and Kike Turrón (2020),[15] was well received by critics and has led to numerous articles on the role of Los Rodríguez in Spanish rock.

As we have argued throughout these pages, Los Rodríguez have occupied their own space within the synergies of Spanish rock. Art history, cultural studies, musicology and popular music studies have demonstrated the importance of genres and scenes in the creation of artistic ideologies and in the establishment of symbolic boundaries between genres and styles. Los Rodríguez created a place of their own, close to the rock bands of Madrid, but were also attentive to hit songs and pop, rumba and New Flamenco and the hybridizations of rock with indigenous music. For Germán Vilella, the key to the band's identity was its ability to bring together those three universes of rock, pop and fusion:

Songs like 'La Milonga…' and 'Sin documentos' are signature songs of Los Rodríguez. Fortunately, I was wrong, and they ignored me when they showed them to me and I didn't like it. Now I am super happy and proud. But if Los Rodríguez were been a group that only made hybridizations, we would not have been able to maintain the originality of inventing a new formula on each album. Pop songs, like 'Dulce condena', are masterpieces. (Personal communication, 15 June 2019, Figueras)

Some music critics have highlighted the fact that Los Rodríguez made these hybridizations in a rock context that was not favourable for it. For Diego A. Manrique (2020), the value of the group lies in its ability to, in a deeply Anglophile environment like that of Malasaña in the nineties, build a cultural product which was indifferent to such trends:

I suspect that Los Rodríguez were not fully aware of the music that was played in the nineties in Malasaña (a neighbourhood in the centre of Madrid) and that, in those coordinates, they were an anomaly.

We have already seen that some of the music scenes that developed in the Madrid of the nineties, especially around the Malasaña neighbourhood, were marked by a sort of revival of garage rock, punk and hardcore, in such bars as Agapo, while the incipient indie scene, more influenced by noise rock, began to stand out in the Maravillas Club. When Los Rodríguez lived in these environments and moved through these halls and bars, they looked for a musical approach that was closer to Spanish popular culture. Music critic Nando Cruz (2015) shows the Anglophilia of the indie scene in his book *Little Circus*, which suggests that musicians who began to move through the indie scene sought to separate themselves from the legacy of the scenes of the eighties, such as *La Movida Madrileña*. We have already seen that *La Movida Madrileña* has been criticized and problematized for its elitism and apoliticism, but it is undeniable that some of the bands related to that scene (Gabinete Caligari, Radio Futura, Los Coyotes, Kiko Veneno and Alaska y Dinarama) transferred pop-rock to their own cultural coordinates and managed to make their music popular, broadcast, played and consumed, not only by the most avant-garde fans but by the average listener as well. In that sense, Los Rodríguez achieved something similar. For David Bonilla,

> Los Rodríguez were a rock band like no other in Spain. They had a Latin American touch, which at that time was very fashionable, but also quite reviled, because the indie scene attacked everything that sounded Latino. And they had the Latin American touch, obviously because of the origin of Andrés and Ariel, and because they found a sound that worked and was natural to them. (Personal communication, 29 September 2019, Madrid)

According to Kike Babas, biographer of the group:

> Los Rodríguez were one of the essential bands to understand rock in Spain, as Miguel Ríos could have been before. This is a band that reintroduced rock into homes. They were liked by the little brother and the mother. They frequented all the town squares and outdoor festivals. (In Carmona 2020)

A clear sign of the importance of Los Rodríguez, and of their impact on Spanish popular music, is that after their separation in 1996, some of the music that emerged within the world of pop-rock was influenced by the group's triple facets. For Germán Vilella,

> when Los Rodríguez split, I left Spain and returned five years later. On the way back, I found Estopa, El Canto del Loco, La Cabra Mecánica and Pereza, which reminded me of our songs. However, I don't think it was because we created a school, but because we unified several schools: the groups that flirted with Latin sounds, the ones that made pop and the ones that did rock. Andrés Calamaro's singing style is also important, as it was quite new in Spain, although it already existed in Argentina. Andrés took the most lyrical, tuneful and graceful singing style from there and added a flatter, more rock-like style, with a touch of Spain, and that's what a lot of people here have imitated. For me, singers like Leiva, for example, are part of the Calamaro school. (Personal communication, 15 June 2019, Figueras)

David Bonilla also points out that, after Los Rodríguez broke up, many of the new bands that emerged had connections to them.

> There were many bands with that flair. I remember many demos that sounded like them. There's a lot of rock groups that I don't know whether they sound like Los Rodríguez or like the way Andrés Calamaro sings. Los Rodríguez were a 'before and after' in rock in Spain, without any doubt. They were the first to gain visibility for their combination of rock with a sort of rumba and with Latin American sounds. There was a mix of rock with something Latin that worked very well. (Personal communication, 29 September 2019, Madrid)

Although there are some groups that, both musically and aesthetically, were clearly inspired by Los Rodríguez (like El Hombre Gancho), we argue that Los Rodríguez generated a sound – certain ways of writing, singing and performing songs – that influenced many groups that appeared a few years later. On the one hand, rumba, Latin roots music and related genres begin to appear regularly in the repertoire of Spanish pop-rock groups. Successful examples of this influence are such hits as Jarabe de Palo's 1996 'La flaca' (Skinny Woman), La Cabra Mecánica's 2000 'La lista de la compra' (Shopping List), El Canto del Loco's 2003 'La madre de José (José's Mother),[16] and Joaquín Sabina's 1999 '19 días y 500 noches' (19 Days and 500 Nights), as well as Estopa's debut album (2000). Although we could cite other artists and genres that have influenced each of these artists, such as Hombres G, Manu Chao, Extremoduro, Bambino and Los Chichos, we propose that the success of Los Rodríguez and their hybridized style paved the way and legitimized a form of understanding pop-rock that was accepted by critics, the industry and the public.

Undoubtedly, part of this lasting influence is due to the personality and singing style of Andrés Calamaro. While Ariel Rot is an established and respected musician in Spain, Calamaro has become a character loved by fans and constantly covered by the press because he always provides juicy statements. In musical terms, Calamaro's landing in Spanish popular music opened the way for the acceptance of other Latin American musicians on the national scene, such as Coti, Andy Chango, Jorge Drexler and Julieta Venegas. The familiarity with which critics and audiences have embraced these artists' albums and attended their concerts would not be the same without the initial push from Calamaro, and from Los Rodríguez in general.

As music critic Fernando Navarro (2019) has put it, 'Calamaro is a genre unto himself.' The path exploring Latin genres, from bolero to tango, from ranchera to candombe, has been extended in his most recent works. However, no matter what style he composes in, Calamaro always imposes his personality on the music through his singing, which is influenced by the theatricality of tango as well as the decadence of rock. He can drag his voice into slow tracks like 'Especies que desaparecen' to convey total despair or cause a summer fire with 'Mucho mejor'. He can sound sweet on the most pop-like songs and rasp while emulating the Rolling Stones. He can make clever references to Dylan and insert them into an everyday atmosphere. Calamaro's voice is always at the service of the song, but all the songs are at the service of the ego of the artist, who treats songs as pages of a journal that he quickly shares with his followers. Part of Calamaro's success can possibly be attributed to the transparency and immediacy that he transmitted to his fans. The theatricality of Calamaro's voice always positions himself as the protagonist, always reclaims the brand of authenticity, always expresses profound feelings and never forgets that it drinks from both classic rock and the torrent of Spanish and Latin American genres that have crossed paths in his life.

Conclusions

The story of Los Rodríguez is just one chapter in a longer tale that has been told only partially, focusing on the rock exchanges between Spain and Latin America and their intersection with global hybridization trends in popular music. Therefore, more so than drawing conclusions, this book proposes lines of inquiry for future research that outline some of the ideas from the previous pages.

One of the preliminary issues for locating the impact of Los Rodríguez on Spanish-language rock is the different status that rock has had in the national cultures of each of the two countries. The importance of national rock in Argentina, the existence of a canon of consecrated artists and the insertion of rock in the fields of culture and politics have endowed Argentine musicians with tremendous symbolic capital when they circulate throughout Latin America. Throughout the book, there have been many examples of praise for the ability of Argentine musicians to create messages that permeate society as a whole and to make Spanish sound like a natural language of rock, as well as for their technical prowess. At this point, it should be noted that this expertise is valued in two directions: on the one hand, their knowledge of the canon of international rock and the ability to make it their own, and on the other, their ability to handle other sound sources beyond rock and integrate them into a production that sounds both unequivocally rock and clearly Latin American. Calamaro's experience with candombe before joining Los Abuelos de la Nada, his taste for celebratory songs typical of the Mexican ranchera and the indelible imprint of tango on the most sentimental songs are good examples of this musical integration that is undoubtedly at the foundation of the influence of Los Rodríguez. This is particularly true when combined with their endless references to the work of Bob Dylan (especially in the lyrics) and to the Rolling Stones and Faces (especially in playing and recording electric guitars).

In contrast, Spanish rock has not had such a deep cultural imprint. Los Rodríguez began playing in Madrid after the end of *La Movida Madrileña*, an unusual moment in Spanish culture in which popular music (pop more so than rock) was at the centre of the cultural stage. However, beyond the eighties, popular music has had a peripheral role in the Spanish cultural realm, where writers and film-makers have always been the main figures. In addition, as we have seen, Los Rodríguez burst onto the Spanish music scene at a time when rock's relationship with the Spanish popular musical tradition was in a process of renegotiation: while albums and songs with an enormous presence of rumba and flamenco sounds succeeded at the popular level, critics placed a higher value on the sound of indie groups, whose influences were entirely English-speaking contemporary bands.

However, the combination of 'Spanishized' Argentines (Rot after his time in Tequila), native Spaniards (Infante and Vilella) and newly arrived Argentines (Calamaro) is what generated the distinctive sound of Los Rodríguez and their subsequent influence. Despite Julián Infante's rhythmic ability to play rumba and Germán Vilella's experience with New Flamenco, it was Calamaro's musical restlessness (and possibly his friendship with Antonio Flores, who introduced him to Madrid's flamenco world) that installed rumba in the sound of Los Rodríguez (first in 'Engánchate conmigo', then in 'Sin Documentos').

As we have pointed out in the previous chapters, when musicians are forced to live between two cultures, they tend to adapt their original cultural and musical background to the new environment in which they have settled. Los Rodríguez always wanted to be a Madrid band: Rot, despite his Argentine origins, had managed to carve out his reputation as a musician during his time in Madrid with Tequila. Los Rodríguez settled into the rehearsal rooms of Tablada Street and its surrounding local community, which was in transformation. The classics of *La Movida Madrileña* (Gabinete Caligari) coincided there with younger bands (such as Los Ronaldos), while Los Rodríguez coexisted in the Malasaña nights with a younger generation that shared their taste for classic rock, but not their commitment to the Spanish language.

As we have pointed out, this game of mirrors in which a musical tradition is constantly revised by an external gaze has been a constant in the way Spaniards have related to their musical tradition. The foreigner, a stranger to the local culture, is the one who can value the elements of the local tradition. Calamaro's admiration for flamenco and bullfighting is reminiscent of the first romantic travellers and their fascination with fandango. In the case of Calamaro, however, his admiration is combined with the legacy of a powerful tradition, Argentina's national rock, which came to function as a toolbox that allowed him to integrate any foreign sounds within rock music without any problems.

Although we have not dwelt too much on this point, it should be noted that this game of mirrors has one more element: the presence of English producers on Los Rodríguez's hit albums, which was shared by other contemporary groups that were looking for a more Latin American sound. It is striking that this Latin touch did not come from the hands of Latin American producers. It is as if the involvement of producers from an external culture made it the groups themselves who delimited the integration of Latin American elements. As an example, it is worth mentioning that Los Rodríguez rejected the wind arrangements that producer Joe Blaney had commissioned for *Palabras más, palabras menos*, the album they put out after *Sin Documentos*, because they considered the arrangements to be too close to salsa.

Throughout this book, we have emphasized that the success of Los Rodríguez was based on the combined talents of its four members: no matter how much Calamaro has claimed the composition of the song 'Sin Documentos', it was Vilella's rhythmic contribution that gave it the unmistakable tone that made it a hit. Certainly, Andrés Calamaro was an essential component in defining the tone of the band's songs, not only because of his singing style, which fed on Dylan and tango simultaneously, but also because of his distinctive emotional approach. Ariel Rot's compositions tended to have a feel-good and festive tone, while Calamaro's compositions, even when they were rhythmically more powerful, always had a trace of dissatisfaction, doubt and fear. Calamaro, as we have pointed out, introduced to Spanish rock the archetype of the suffering man, which might have originated in the tango scene but was alien to the rock tradition. Singer-songwriters, flamenco performers and ballad singers had all suffered from a broken heart, and now, thanks to Calamaro's contribution, so do rockers.

The integration of costumbrist elements in his songs is another one of Calamaro's contributions as a lyricist. Following Moris's legacy by joining forces with a skilled rock singer-songwriter like Sabina, Los Rodríguez created songs that simultaneously transmitted the cosmopolitan flair that immigrants always bring to their host societies and the local flavour of the characters representative of the Madrid of the nineties, like employees at El Corte Inglés and subscribers of Canal Plus.

Sin Documentos, with all its complexities, has given us an opportunity to examine the decade of the nineties in Spain. After the euphoria of the Spanish Transition to democracy in the eighties, the last decade of the twentieth century ended with Spain seeming like something of an exception in the European context: the country was opened to foreign investment, old monopolies (such as television) were broken and cities became more diverse with the arrival of immigrants from all over the world. That same openness and diversity, which reflected global dynamics, resonated in the work of Los Rodríguez – a band created between two nations separated by an ocean, heir to a rock tradition that marked the culture of the entire second half of the twentieth century, inserted into a city in transformation that had one eye on globalization and the other on the Spanish tradition. The genius of Los Rodríguez was to compose and record a handful of songs that use catchy melodies and rock riffs to express the complexities of an era.

Notes

Introduction

1   José Luís López Vazquez was a very well-known Spanish
    actor. He participated in some iconic films of Spanish cinema
    such as *El pisito* (1959), *Plácido* (1961), *Mi querida señorita*
    (1971) or *La escopeta nacional* (1978), and has been valued for
    representing the average Spanish citizen during Francoism on
    his performances.

2   The term 'costumbrismo' refers to an artistic trend, rooted in
    Spain, focused on portraying typical uses and customs.

3   A charming bar located in Madrid's Malasaña neighbourhood.

4   The historical period between the death of dictator Francisco
    Franco in 1975 and the consolidation of democracy in Spain
    is called *Transición* (Transition). There is still an open debate
    between historians and cultural critics to determine the
    moment in which the Transition was finished, although many
    argue for 1982, when the Socialist Party, repressed during the
    dictatorship, came into government.

5   The album was ranked number 61 on *Rockdelux*'s list of the
    100 best Spanish records from the twentieth century and
    number 29 on *EfeEme*'s list of the 200 best Spanish pop
    albums. Two songs from the album, 'Sin Documentos' and
    'Dulce condena', were included on *Rolling Stone*'s list of 200
    greatest Spanish pop-rock songs, ranking twenty-second and
    fifty-ninth, respectively.

6 *Verbenas* are local, traditional, outdoor, often religion-related festivities and festivals that are typically celebrated in Spain.

7 In Spain, Portugal and other Latin American countries, a *tuna* is a group of university students who play traditional instruments, such as lute, guitar, bandurria and tambourine, in traditional university dress consisting of a cloak, doublet, shirt and stockings.

8 Sardana is a musical genre typical of Catalan culture and danced in circle following a set of steps.

9 *Quejíos* or *quejidos* are a series of distressing and prolonged moans typically incorporated in flamenco music.

10 *Pasodoble* (double step) is a march-like military genre with a binary rhythm, often played in bullfighting and local celebrations and festivals.

11 Miguel de Unamuno was one of the most important writers of the so-called Generation of 1898; these writers' books discuss extensively the role of Spain in the world after the loss of the last colonies in 1898.

12 Bands like La Polla Records and Eskorbuto are well known in Chile and Perú for their contribution to the popularization of Spanish punk in those countries, in contexts in which military dictatorships and authoritarian governments complicated the arrival of those music genres (Canales Cabrera 2017).

1 Sin Documentos

1 As Pablo Alabarces (1992: 39) points out, Los Teen Tops were well known in Argentina, so it was not only in Spain that Latin American groups disseminated rock music.

2   TVE, the public broadcasting service, had a monopoly on TV
    broadcasts until the end of the eighties, when regional public
    channels were opened. The first private TV channel started to
    air in 1990.

3   Diego Manrique, Juan Puchades and Jesús Ordovás have paid
    close attention to the impact of Argentine rock in Spain. See
    EfeEme (2019).

4   Gatti later worked with CBS Records on designs for Mecano
    and Alaska y Dinarama. He is best known in Spain for his work
    with Pedro Almodóvar.

5   Ordovás refers here to the list of Los 40 Principales, the main
    music radio network in Spain.

6   Sergio Makaroff is another Argentine musician who settled
    in Spain in the late seventies. He has composed songs and
    worked with Ariel Rot, Andrés Calamaro and Los Rodríguez, in
    addition to having developed his musical career in Spain.

7   Phrases from the song 'Este Madrid', by the urban rock
    group Leño.

8   Casa de Campo is the largest public park in Madrid.

9   Tequila has had a second era, starting in 2008, but with only
    two of the original members, Alejo Stivel and Ariel Rot, and
    with hardly any new material.

2 Mi Rock Perdido

1   The Barcelona model that starts with the Olympic Games has
    been widely studied and criticized (Delgado 2007).

2   *Copla*, or *copla andaluza*, is a Spanish music genre, related
    to other genres such as *cuplé* or *tonadilla*, which was very
    popular in Spain from 1930 to 1960. Lyrics deal with such
    issues as love, disappointment and jealousy.

3   The website for these rehearsal rooms, which is still active,
    features an autographed photo of Los Rodríguez at the door
    to one of the rehearsal rooms.

4   Statements made in an interview with Arancha Moreno,
    available at https://www.youtube.com/watch?v=CvG5
    ihmx9jU.

5   Siroco is a mythical concert hall, located in Madrid's Malasaña
    neighbourhood, where Los Rodríguez performed their first
    concerts.

6   This influence was made explicit in the lyrics of the song
    'Aquellos besos' (Those Kisses), featured on his solo album
    Honestidad brutal (Brutal Honesty).

7   Head of A&R at Warner Music, worked with Los Rodríguez,
    especially from their album *Palabras más, palabras menos*
    (1995). Statements obtained in a personal interview (Madrid,
    29 September 2019).

8   Coinciding with the break-up of Los Rodríguez, DRO Records
    put out a tribute album to Tequila (*Mucho Tequila*, 1997), and
    BMG released a compilation album (*Tequila Forever*, 1999) and
    reissued albums in CD format.

3 Pequeño Salto Mortal

1   German Vilella's biography and memories were obtained via
    personal communication (Figueras, 15 June 2019).

2   This song was later included on *Sin Documentos*.

3   The distinction between pop and rock is always controversial. In this case, we define as pop those songs with clear melodies and a catchy chorus.

4   According to the group's biography, it is clear that there was a certain tension between Martín and Los Rodríguez. When the band first started, guitarist Guillermo Martín, Fernando's brother and also a member of Desperados, assumed the position of bass guitar in the group, taking care of that instrument on the recording of the album. But at one point, Fernando pressured his brother to focus on Desperados and leave Los Rodríguez. From there, Los Rodríguez had a strange relationship with its bassists. Several men performed this role (Daniel Zamora, Candy Avelló) but none was ever credited as a permanent member of the band.

5   The term 'Caño Roto sound' was used in the seventies to designate groups that were mainly produced by José Luís de Carlos and fused progressive and psychedelic rock with flamenco and rumba, such as Las Grecas and Los Chorbos, as well as groups more connected to rumba, such as Los Chichos and Los Chunguitos.

6   However, neither 'Chiquilla' nor Seguridad Social has been vindicated by critics, and they do not appear in some of the lists of best Spanish pop-rock artists made by the specialized press (*Rockdelux, Rolling Stone, EfeEme*). As we will see later, Los Rodríguez did enter into this process of canonization.

7   We thank musicologist and guitarist Paco Bethencourt for his explanations and help in understanding the structure of these songs.

8 *Ventilador* is a guitar technique typical of *rumba catalana* that combines percussion on the body of the guitar and fast chord changes.

9 *Payo* is a term used by gypsies to refer to non-gypsy people.

10 These are different flamenco styles.

11 Julián Infante's reluctance to accept the group's rumba has also been explained by Rot (in Puchades 2003: 129), who pointed out that Calamaro said to Infante, when showing him the song 'Engánchate conmigo' from the first album: 'I'm going to leave you a wad of cash on top of the amplifier.' Again, we can see the presence of economic issues in the band's stories.

12 The Argentine leg of the tour was depicted in the documentary *100 pájaros volando* (100 Birds Flying).

13 http://lafonoteca.net/disco/sin-documentos.

14 https://www.rtve.es/television/la-mejor-cancion-jamas-cantada/.

15 Musicians, writers and journalists Babas and Turrón have become the biographers of many Spanish rock stars, authoring books on some of the most relevant bands of the country, such as Siniestro Total, Leño, Manu Chao, Reincidentes, Rosendo, Boikot and Los Enemigos.

16 In a sort of self-parody tribute, El Canto del Loco included a cover of *Sin Documentos*, on their album *Radio La Colifata*, in which they merged the song with their own 'La madre de José', recognizing the enormous influence of Los Rodríguez on their song.

References

Abello Onofre, C. (2018), 'Scratching the Stones of Rock and Roll: Love Lyrics in the Times of the Argentinian Dictatorship', *Rock Music Studies*, 5 (1): 76–93.

Alabarces, P. (1992), *Entre Gatos y Violadores: El rock nacional en la cultura argentina*, Buenos Aires: Colihue.

Alonso, C., ed. (2010), *Creación musical, cultura popular y construcción nacional en la España contemporánea*, Madrid: ICCMU.

Arnáiz, J. (1978), 'Moris, un rockero clásico', *Ozono*, 35: 55–6.

Babas, K., and K. Turrón (2004), *Tremendo delirio: Conversaciones con Julián Hernández y biografía de Siniestro total*, Madrid: Fundación Autor.

Babas, K., and K. Turrón (2020), *Sol y sombra: Los Rodríguez*, Bilbao: BAO Bilbao Ediciones.

Bermúdez, S. (2018), *Rocking the Boat: Migration and Race in Contemporary Spanish Music*, Toronto: University of Toronto Press.

Born, G. (2005), 'On Musical Mediation: Ontology, Technology and Creativity', *Twentieth-Century Music*, 2 (1): 7–36.

Canales Cabrera, J. (2017), *Diez años de punk en Chile: De los circuitos del underground artístico a la autogestión*, Santiago de Chile: Universidad Alberto Hurtado.

Carmona, J. (2020), 'Los Rodríguez, la banda que tardó en conquistar España', *Público*, 8 November. Available online: https://www.publico.es/culturas/rodrig uez-banda-tardo-conquistar-espana.html (accessed 2 June 2021).

Casares, E., ed. (1999), *Diccionario de la Música Española e Hispanoamericana*, Madrid: Fundación Autor.

Constenla, T. (2000), 'Vecinos de El Ejido armados con barras de hierro atacan a los inmigrantes y destrozan sus locales', *El País*, 7 February. Available online: https://elpais.com/dia rio/2000/02/07/espana/949878022_850215.html (accessed 3 June 2021).

Corazón Rural, Á. (2018), 'Ariel Rot: Los nuevos grupos de rock son muy profesionales, parecen boy scouts', *Jot Down*, November. Available online: https://www.jotdown.es/2018/11/ ariel-rot-los-nuevos-grupos-de-rock-son-muy-profesionales- parecen-boy-scouts/ (accessed 20 May 2021).

Cruz, N. (2015), *Pequeño circo: Historia oral del indie en España*, Barcelona: Contra.

Delgado, M. (2007), *La ciudad mentirosa: Fraude y miseria del 'modelo Barcelona'*, Madrid: Los Libros de la Catarata.

Domínguez, S. (2002), *Bienvenido Mr. Rock: Los primeros grupos hispanos (1957–1975)*, Madrid: Fundación Autor.

Domínguez, S. (2004), *Los hijos del rock: Los grupos hispanos (1975– 1989)*, Madrid: Fundación Autor.

EfeEme (2019), *Cuadernos EfeEme 3: Special Issue Tequila.* Madrid: EfeEme.

Faulín, I. (2016), *Bienvenido Mr. USA: La música norteamericana en España antes del rock and roll, 1865–1955*, Lleida: Milenio.

Flamencopolis (2021), *Rumba*. Available online: https://www. flamencopolis.com/archives/300 (accessed 21 June 2021).

Fouce, H. (2007), *El futuro ya está aquí: Música pop y cambio cultural 1978–1985*, Madrid: Velecío.

Fouce, H., and J. Pecourt (2008), 'Emociones en lugar de soluciones: Intelectuales y cambio político en la España de la Transición', *Trans*, 12. Available online: https://www.sibetr ans.com/trans/articulo/105/emociones-en-lugar-de-solucio nes-musica-popular-intelectuales-y-cambio-politico-en-la-esp ana-de-la-transicion (accessed 10 January 2021).

Frith, S. (1981), '"The Magic That Can Set You Free": The Ideology of Folk and the Myth of the Rock Community', *Popular Music*, 1: 159–68.

Frith, S. (1999), 'La constitución de la música rock como industria transnacional', in G. Talens (ed.), *Las culturas del rock*, 11–30, Valencia: Pre-textos.

García Peinazo, D. (2017), *Rock Andaluz: Significación musical, identidades e ideología en la España del tardofranquismo y la transición*, Madrid: SEDEM.

García Salueña, E. (2017), *Música para la libertad: Nuevas tecnologías, experimentación y procesos de fusión en el rock progresivo de la España de la Transición: el eje noroeste*, Barcelona: Norte Sur.

González Férriz, R. (2020), *La trampa del optimismo: Como los años noventa explican el mundo actual*, Madrid: Debate.

Grossberg, L. (1993), 'The Media Economy of Rock Culture: Cinema, Post-modernity and Authenticity', in S. Frith, A. Goodwin and L. Grossber (eds) *Sound and Vision: The Music Video Reader*, 185–209, London: Routledge.

Iglesias, I. (2017), *La modernidad elusiva: Jazz, baile y política en la Guerra Civil española y el franquismo, 1936–1968*, Madrid: CSIC.

I.N.E (Instituto Nacional de Estadística) (2020), *Cifras de población*. Available online: https://www.ine.es/dyngs/INEb ase/es/operacion.htm?c=Estadistica_C&cid=1254736176 951&menu=ultiDatos&idp=1254735572981 (accessed 3 March 2021).

Iñiguez, F. (1993), 'La Sangre Española de Manolo Tena vuelve a correr por Madrid', *El País*, 22 December. Available online: https://elpais.com/diario/1993/12/22/madrid/75656 3085_850215.html.

JOB (1978), '*Tequila: rocanrol atractivo*', *Disco Express*, 480: 12–13.

Keightley, K. (2006), 'Reconsiderar el rock', in S. Frith, W. Straw and J. Street (eds), *La otra historia del rock*, trans. J. Conde, 155–94, Barcelona: Ediciones Robinbook.

Larocca, B. (2018), 'Los Rodríguez: La historia de 'Sin documentos', el disco que dio vuelta el rock en español', *La Nación*, 3 September. Available online: https://www.lanacion.com.ar/espectaculos/musica/los-rodriguez-la-historia-de-sin-documentos-el-disco-que-dio-vuelta-el-rock-en-espanol-nid2167665/ (accessed 20 October 2020).

Lesende, T., and F. Neira (2006), *201 discos para engancharse al pop-rock español*, Madrid: Fundación Autor.

Manrique, D. (2014), *Honestidad brutal. O la huida hacia delante de Andrés Calamaro.* Madrid: Lengua de Trapo.

Manrique, D. A. (1995), *Tequila: Historia.* Available online: https://tequilamania.tripod.com/princ/histo/hist1.html (accessed 22 June 2021).

Manrique, D. A. (2000), 'Échate un cantecito', *El País*, 21 August. Available online: https://elpais.com/diario/2000/08/21/revistaverano/966808836_850215.htm.

Manrique, D. A. (2019), 'El comando argentino', in *Cuadernos EfeEme* 3: 15–17.

Manrique, D. A. (2020), 'Revolución en Malasaña', *El País*, 11 October. Available online: https://elpais.com/cultura/2020-10-11/los-rodriguez-la-vida-intima-y-la-muerte-prematura-del-rock-que-reino-en-la-espana-euforica.html (accessed 15 March 2021).

Manrique, D. A., and M. Cuellar (2009), 'Felicidades, rock', *El País*, 27 September. Available online: https://elpais.com/diario/2009/09/27/eps/1254032813_850215.html (accessed 17 February 2021).

Marc, I. (2013), 'Submarinos amarillos: Transcultural Objects in Spanish Popular Music during Late Francoism', in S. Martínez and H. Fouce (eds), *Made in Spain: Studies in Popular Music*, 115–24, Lonndon: Routledge.

Márquez, F. (1981), *Música Moderna*, Madrid: La banda de Moebius.

Martínez Arhens, J. (1995), 'Una docena de bandas de rapados copa la violencia de las tribus urbanas', *El País*, 15 August. Available online: https://elpais.com/diario/1995/08/15/mad rid/808485873_850215.html (accessed 14 April 2021).

Mira, G. (2005), '¿Por qué se fueron, por qué se van? Migraciones y exilios en la Argentina contemporánea', in *Migraciones: Claves del intercambio entre Argentina y España*, 176–210, Madrid: Siglo XXI.

Mostaza, G. (2016), 'De Ley, de Rosario, obra maestra del mainstream patrio', *Jenesaispop*, 2 September. Available online: https://jenesaispop.com/2016/09/02/274401/ de-ley-de-rosario-obra-maestra-del-mainstream-patrio/ (accessed 26 April 2021).

Navarro, F. (2019), 'Andrés Calamaro, un pirata intratable', *El País*, 28 June. Available online: https://elpais.com/cultura/2019/06/28/ actualidad/1561732040_338091.html (accessed 6 June 2021).

Ogas, J. (2019), 'Identidad sonora y exilio: Roque Narvaja y Moris en España', *Cuadernos de Etnomusicología*, 13.

Ordovás, J. (1987), *Historia del pop español*, Madrid: Alianza.

Ordovás, J. (2010), *Los discos esenciales del pop español*, Madrid: Lunwerg.

Osvaldo Esteban, F. (2015), *El sueño de los perdedores; cuatro décadas de inmigración argentina en España*, Buenos Aires: Teseo.

Pardo, J. R. (2005), *Historia del pop español*, Madrid: Rama Lama Music.

Pedro, J. (2021), *El blues en España: Hibridación y diversidad cultural desde los orígenes al auge de le escena madrileña*, Valencia: Tirant lo Blanc.

Puchades, J. (2003), *Sin vuelta atrás: Conversaciones con Ariel Rot*, Madrid: Fundación Autor.

Puchades, J. (2007), 'Moris: El fundador del rock en nuestro idioma', *EfeEme*, 11 July. Available online: https://www.efe

eme.com/moris-el-fundador-del-rock-en-nuestro-idioma/ (accessed 9 January 2021).

Puchades, J. (2008a), 'El largo viaje del pop español', *El País*, 20 December. Available online: https://elpais.com/dia rio/2008/12/20/babelia/1229733553_850215.html (accessed 6 November 2020).

Puchades, J. (2008b), 'La fiebre contagiosa del rock en español', *El País*, 23 August. Available online: https://elpais.com/dia rio/2008/08/23/babelia/1219446372_850215.html (accessed 26 November 2020).

Puchades, J. (2011), *Peret, biografía de la rumba*, Barcelona: Global Rythms.

Pujol, S. (2015), 'Escúchame, alúmbrame: Apuntes sobre el canon de "la música joven" argentina entre 1966 y 1973', *Apuntes de investigación del CECYP*, 25: 11–25.

Regev, M. (2013), *Pop-Rock Music: Aesthetic Cosmopolitanism in Late Modernity*, Cambridge: Polity Press.

Roa Bastos, A. (1991), 'El controvertido V centenario', *El País*, 18 June. Available online: https://elpais.com/diario/1991/06/18/ opinion/677196008_850215.html (accessed 8 March 2021).

Sabina, J., and J. Menéndez Flórez (2008), *Sabina en carne viva*, Barcelona: Random House.

Secul Giusti, C. (2016), *Rompiendo el silencio: La construcción discursiva de la libertad en las líricas de rock-pop argentino durante el período 1982–1989*, La Plata: Universidad de La Plata.

Shain, R. M. (2012), 'Trovador of the Black Atlantic: Laba Sosseh and the Africanization of Afro-Cuban Music', in B. W. White (ed.), *Music and Globalization: Critical Encounters*, 135–56, Bloomington: Indiana University Press.

Val Ripollés, F. (2017), *Rockeros insurgentes, modernos complacientes: Un análisis sociológico del rock en la Transición (1975–1985)*, Madrid: Fundación SGAE.

Vila, P. (1985), 'Rock nacional, crónicas de la resistencia juvenil',
    in E. Jelin (ed.), *Los nuevos movimientos sociales: Mujeres, rock
    nacional*, 83–156, Buenos Aires: CEAL.

Vilarós, T. (1998), *El mono del desencanto: Una crítica cultural de la
    transición española (1973–1993)*, Madrid: Siglo XXI.

Viñuela, E. (2019), 'Rock en español: Un terreno de disputa y
    convergencia entre España y Latinoamérica', *Resonancias*, 23
    (45): 197–214.

Vogel, A. (2017), *Bikinis, fútbol y rock&roll: Crónica pop bajo el
    franquismo sociológico (1950–1977)*, Madrid: Foca.

Wheeler, D. (2016), 'You've Got to Fight for Your Right to Party?
    Spanish Punk Rockers and Democratic Values', *Popular Music
    and Society*, 41 (2): 132–53.

Index